'Jacky Newcomb, The Angel Lady – the world's leading expert on all things paranormal – shares her knowledge in an exciting, inspiring, easy style. Jacky is a warm and loving angelic envoy [who] predicted two and a half years ago that my book would be published and successful ... she was right. Let her light and inspire you as she did me.'
Joylina Goodings, internationally renowned TV and media spiritual consultant, teacher and author of *Your Angel Journey*

'... Jacky is the UK's leading author on Angels ...'
Spiritual ConneXtions.com

'Jacky – this world is a better place because you are in it, thanks from my heart ... you are an angel.'
Barbara Meiklejohn-Free, 'The Highland Seer' and author of *The Heart of All Knowing: awakening your inner seer*

'Many people have paranormal experiences. Jacky Newcomb explains the phenomenon in an easy-to-understand, non-threatening way.'
Jordan McAuley, ContactAnyCelebrity.com

'Jacky Newcomb's extensive knowledge is generously passed to the reader like drops of liquid gold ...'
Jenny Smedley, TV presenter and author of *Pets Have Souls Too*

'Jacky Newcomb is a warm and spectacular person ... extremely inspirational and gifted ... Her spark ignites even the most sceptical of hearts and a moment in her company makes you feel like you have been touched by someone very special.'
Laura Wells, editor of *The Psychic Voice*

Dear Angel Lady

Dear Angel Lady

Jacky Newcomb
THE ANGEL LADY

HAY HOUSE

HAY HOUSE
Australia • Canada • Hong Kong • India
South Africa • United Kingdom • United States

First published and distributed in the United Kingdom by:
Hay House UK Ltd, 292B Kensal Rd, London W10 5BE. Tel.: (44) 20 8962 1230; Fax: (44) 20 8962 1239. www.hayhouse.co.uk

Published and distributed in the United States of America by:
Hay House, Inc., PO Box 5100, Carlsbad, CA 92018-5100. Tel.: (1) 760 431 7695 or (800) 654 5126; Fax: (1) 760 431 6948 or (800) 650 5115. www.hayhouse.com

Published and distributed in Australia by:
Hay House Australia Ltd, 18/36 Ralph St, Alexandria NSW 2015. Tel.: (61) 2 9669 4299; Fax: (61) 2 9669 4144. www.hayhouse.com.au

Published and distributed in the Republic of South Africa by:
Hay House SA (Pty), Ltd, PO Box 990, Witkoppen 2068. Tel./Fax: (27) 11 467 8904. www.hayhouse.co.za

Published and distributed in India by:
Hay House Publishers India, Muskaan Complex, Plot No.3, B-2, Vasant Kunj, New Delhi – 110 070. Tel.: (91) 11 4176 1620; Fax: (91) 11 4176 1630. www.hayhouse.co.in

Distributed in Canada by:
Raincoast, 9050 Shaughnessy St, Vancouver, BC V6P 6E5. Tel.: (1) 604 323 7100; Fax: (1) 604 323 2600

The author of this book does not dispense medical advice or prescribe the use of any technique as a form of treatment for physical or medical problems without the advice of a physician, either directly or indirectly. The intent of the author is only to offer information of a general nature to help you in your quest for emotional and spiritual wellbeing. In the event you use any of the information in this book for yourself, which is your constitutional right, the author and the publisher assume no responsibility for your actions.

A catalogue record for this book is available from the British Library.

ISBN 978-1-84850-064-8

Printed in the UK by CPI Bookmarque, Croydon, CR0 4TD.

To Mum

I'm so proud of you and how you have handled this past year, and Dad would be proud of you, too. Thank you for always being the angel by my side.

Jacky x

Contents

Acknowledgements

As usual I would like to thank everyone at my publishers Hay House, especially Jo and Michelle, the sales team and everyone who helped with everything from the layout to spell-checking and cover design! These books would never happen without you and I appreciate everything you do – even when (and especially when) I am so bossy about checking every little detail! Thank you, Liz, my literary agent, who keeps me on the straight and narrow.

I think it's always most important to remember YOU the reader. Your stories make each and every book unique. Thank you for continuing to support me in every way. I know I have the best fans in the world.

The Robin – a poem

There's a Robin that taps on my window
He seems to have something to say
He visits me every morning
Before he goes on his way.
A Robin visits my garden
He seems to know when and where
I feel like he brings me a message
And always knows I'll be there.
The Robin feels so familiar
I'm sure he's bringing a sign
The way he moves and the way he acts
It seems like something divine.
Maybe the Robin's from heaven
A messenger sent from above
Making it clear that everything's fine
And bringing the gift of love.
The Robin picks up my sadness
The Robin feels my pain
But now that I've got his message
I hope he still comes back again.

Introduction

Dear Angel Lady is my ninth published work and the one I am most excited about.

I receive many thousands of emails and letters each year from all over the world, and this book gives me the opportunity of answering some of your many questions about angels and the afterlife. Regular readers are also interested in my own adventures and psychic experiences, so I've updated you on the latest here.

One of the biggest changes in my personal life is the loss of my dear dad, Ron Hill, who passed away just as I finished my last book. I'm excited to tell you that Dad has stayed close and is now helping me with my work from the other side of life … and he's not the only one (but more of that later).

As usual there are stacks more of your stories of angels and the afterlife. Just when I think I know everything there is to know, I get a whole new collection of letters which gives me more information and I can't wait to share my insights with you! I love my job!

Enjoy!

Part I

Chapter 1

Angel Lady

'I'm no angel, but I've spread my wings a bit.'
Mae West

GUARDIAN ANGEL-DAD

'Hello, Dad, why are you here? Don't you know you're dead?' I said as my father stood in front of me.

Dad passed over in February 2008 … but he was still alive, at least his spirit was alive. Dad had physically died but in every other way he continued to exist.

Dad was visiting in what experts call a 'dream visitation'. My body was asleep but my mind was wide awake, totally lucid and aware of what was happening.

This was no ordinary dream. Familiar with dream visitations for many years, I was already expecting, anticipating, a visit from Dad after he passed over to the other side of life … heaven … but I still wanted to check he knew he was dead. He did! Dad laughed and gave his usual 'thumbs up' sign. As in life, his appearance was filled with joy.

After his death Dad appeared in many dream-visitations to each of his four daughters. With one daughter he danced, another he hugged … his spirit touch was real and warm. He held our hands and stroked our faces in that loving way he always did in life. Dad's soul had travelled through time and space to connect to his 'little girls'.

He showed us what it was like for him in heaven. He drove his car, he fished, he attended parties … all the things he loved to do when he was alive.

My sisters Dilly (Madeline), Debbie and Diane are all psychic, too, and each of us has lived with psychic experiences and paranormal encounters our whole lives. As four psychic sisters we'd individually had spirit visits from relatives who'd passed over previously … especially Uncle Eric. Eric was a funny man in life and just as humorous after death; his personality remained firmly intact, comforting to his loved ones left behind. Eric paved the way for later contact from Dad.

I remember a momentous conversation with Eric during a séance.

'What do you do all day now, Uncle Eric?'

I have to confess I was expecting a brilliantly 'spiritual' answer that I could pass onto my readers. What I got was a little different: Eric replied, 'I mess around all day!'

Mmmmm – as I said, his humour was still very much as it had been on Earth!

Prediction from My Friend, the Medium and Author, Gordon Smith

Dad's final illness was horrific. He discovered a white mark on his tongue. It looked like a frosted cornflake but was much more ominous. It was diagnosed as cancer. Dad was so frightened of having the operation to remove the cancer from his tongue.

But then I passed on a message I'd received from the TV medium Gordon Smith, a friend, who'd told me kindly, 'Dad will be OK, you know … '

Dad was thrilled with the message and survived the operation, and lived many more months afterwards. Before he passed away, Dad managed a final Christmas with his family, and he and Mum went to see the musical *Joseph and the Amazing Technicolor Dreamcoat* on what turned out to be the last weekend they spent together. Mum and Dad stayed overnight in a London hotel, something they'd never done together in all their years of marriage. What a wonderful memory for Mum: a perfect send-off and a magnificent final weekend of married life.

I feel sure that Gordon's prediction actually helped Dad to fight for those extra months. Because Gordon had said that Dad would be fine, Dad fought to make sure he was.

Reaching Dad with the 'Angel Board'

After Dad passed over, my sisters and I conducted a séance using an angel board (a type of Ouija board or spirit board). Although many people are frightened of this type of tool (and with good reason), we had always used one to reach out to our deceased loved ones. Several members of the family are mediums and psychics, and we are much practised at this reliable method of communicating with the dead. To us it has never been frightening and we've always worked as a family and always in a well-lit room. This is very different to the type of séance you might see on a TV programme where everyone seems to be dressed in black, working by candlelight in a spooky castle trying to summon up some dead king. It makes great TV, but has nothing to do with what we try to achieve.

The board uses a pointer (called a *planchette*) to spell out words using the letters placed around the board in a circle, including the words YES and NO … you've probably seen these. They are often wrongly used for making mischief with spirits (and regularly in the hands of drunken teenagers, if my postbag is anything to go by!) – we use ours only for communicating with loving relatives.

After Dad passed we were all nervous about trying to contact him for the first time. Granted, he'd already visited the family in dream visitations, but this was different. Now we would be able to have a proper conversation.

When my sisters and I finally plucked up the courage to reach him using my angel board, none of us could think of a single thing to say. We didn't know what to ask him! It was a surreal moment. Dad had kept his appointment. He was there in the room as a spirit and we'd no idea what we were going to talk about. I started the communication:

'Dad … how are you?' I faltered, tears in my eyes.

'Dead!' came his amusing reply

You could almost feel him laugh. Of course, what a silly question! Immediately we all began laughing, the ice broken. This was going to be a fun session after all. Dad was a brilliant communicator – via the 'board', light flickering and dream visits among other methods. He was always up to some sort of antics from the other side to let us know he was around.

During another séance I started our session in a similar way, momentarily forgetting our earlier conversation:

'Hi Dad, how are you today?'

'Still dead!' Clearly Dad hadn't forgotten, and once again we all burst out laughing.

UNCLE ERIC … HE WHO LED THE WAY

Before Dad's passing, his brother Eric had led the way … he was the regular visitor in dreams and séances. Our Eric always reminded us of the late British comedian, the brilliantly funny Eric Morecambe. I've loved writing about his spirit antics in several of my previous books.

Dramatically, Uncle Eric once saved Dad's life by passing on valuable information about his health. Eric appeared in a dream visit on that occasion, too, and details of the story (Eric warning me that Dad shouldn't have an operation) were eventually published in the national press. The *Daily Mirror* ran a full-page story about it. Dad lived many more happy years thanks to the help of his deceased brother in heaven.

Eric would flicker lights whenever his name was mentioned, or ring the doorbell with his own special ring (one ring for a spirit visitor – no one physically at the front door, two rings for a living human visitor – get up and answer the bell). Visitors to Mum and Dad's old bungalow were always perplexed when no one was at the door (no one physically, at least) ... but we always knew who it was.

FATHER-IN-LAW JACK ... AS ON EARTH, SO IN HEAVEN

It has always been easy for me to believe in an afterlife, and naturally my own contact with the 'other side' has never been in doubt. Many relatives and family friends have appeared in dream visits over the years, including an old school friend, old family friends and my late father-in-law, Jack, who was a great communicator in life and afterwards.

Jack had been a marketing director for a big brewery in life, and his skill at passing on messages in his work was easily translated to the ability to communicate from the afterlife once he'd passed over. He even passed on messages to my sister – no relation to him – in dreams, because he found her an easy conduit. Jack was able to visit Debbie in dreams because he told her she slept on the 'right vibrational level' … whatever that means! He was a great spirit communicator … bringing regular and useful messages from heaven-side.

Jack was an expert at using the angel board, too, and would spell out his replies painstakingly, letter by letter. Even if you jumped in and 'guessed' what he was saying he'd still continue to spell it all out, right to the end – to ensure there were no mistakes. He was quite fabulous at it!

NOEL EDMONDS BELIEVES IN ANGELS, TOO

My sister Dilly and her family usually went away with Mum and Dad every year, so the first holiday after Dad passed, my husband John and I decided to join them. This way the holiday was a completely new experience for Mum and not the usual holiday … with Dad missing.

We drove to France and stayed in a remote country house. We were right out in the country and it was lovely to be able to hang out around the pool all day and just read books that were not related to work. At last I was able to have a break from working non-stop on my latest book. No one would find me here! How wrong I was …

Every day we would drive out to a large supermarket to fill up the car with lovely French cheeses and wine (naturally, one has to observe the local customs!). It seemed strange to be out of contact with my usual business world, but then one day while we were in the supermarket my telephone rang. It was my agent and she told me that a journalist from the *Daily Express* was trying to get hold of me and could she give them my mobile number? Of course!

I ran out of the shop to get a better signal and the phone rang. Back home in England, TV presenter Noel Edmonds had been talking about his belief in angels and the afterlife, and the newspaper wanted my comments. I could see the rest of the family piling into the car, but all I could do was smile politely and wave. They were all kind enough to wait in the scorching heat as I did the interview standing outside the supermarket – don't anyone let you think my life is all glamour, you know!

Back in England the following day, my sister Diane rushed out to by a copy of the paper which ran the headline, 'I believe in angels – they're guiding all of us.' Noel's face appeared alongside the interview and I was excited that he felt comfortable talking about his experiences, because it helps so many people. I was also grateful that I'd had the opportunity of having my say.

DAD IN FRANCE

That very same night Dad appeared in a dream visitation. Don't ask me how I knew, but I understood that he'd been talking with me for 20 minutes (this was somehow important) and when he said he had to go I begged him to stay a little longer. He disappeared for a moment and came right back again. I felt sure he was trying to show me that he had the spiritual strength to say for long periods of time. Most spirits who visit in dreams can stick around for only a few seconds (more about this later).

Dad and I talked about all sorts of family issues before he finally had to leave. He hugged me in the dream and kissed me goodbye, and as before the experience was totally real. I felt his kiss and I was completely lucid throughout the entire experience. My body was asleep … but my mind was completely awake! His visit was a real one from his spirit.

The following morning sister Dilly was in the kitchen making breakfast when a shadow in the doorway made her jump. The shadow became a figure – it was Dad dressed in his usual holiday attire of shorts, T-shirt, hat and sandals. Typical of the British, Dad always wore socks with his sandals!

No sooner had Dad materialized in a spirit form than he disappeared again. Of course, he always hovered in the doorway at mealtimes when he was alive, so I guess he saw no reason to stop now! Dad was keeping an eye on dinner, letting us know he'd come on holiday, too.

DAD'S DREAM APPEARANCE ON A BUS

One day around ten months after Dad died, I dreamt I was on a double-decker bus. I was sitting on the top level of the bus when Dad appeared in his most solid form yet. His spirit, in a very clear form, walked over to me and we chatted for a long while.

Dad explained that, although he was in regular contact with all of his family on Earth, he was now working with me. He was going to be able to pass on messages from the other side through me for people outside the family.

When I awoke I was excited and for days afterwards I expected that Dad would appear in the same 'solid form' in my waking life! He didn't! I was confused. Wasn't this what he'd meant? What was he trying to say?

The Aftermath of the Dream

Strangely I began to develop a different sort of psychic ability. I was now able to 'read' people in a new and exciting way. After chatting with someone for just a few minutes, I often started picking up information about their future goals and aspirations … their life path. Was Dad passing this information to me? How was I doing this?

A few weeks later my friend, TV medium Barrie John, invited me to a paranormal event he'd organized at Tutbuy Castle. Barrie was a guest medium on TV's *Most Haunted* and I respect his work very much.

Tutbury Castle is in Staffordshire and only a short drive from my home. Custodian Lesley Smith was also present during the evening. She entertained guests dressed as Mary Queen of Scots.

Lesley is quite an icon and another regular on the hit show. I'd worked with her previously when the castle was the venue for a programme called *The World's Biggest Ghost Hunt*. I'd been camera operator and filmed many of the personal paranormal experiences people had during the evening (paranormal experiences being my area of expertise). I also appeared briefly on the show itself, but I noticed when the programme was repeated a few months later they'd cut my section out (thanks, guys! I wasn't that bad was I?!).

It was exciting to be back at Tutbury Castle again – the venue is well known for its ghosts and is a regular venue for ghost-hunt vigils and tours. I kept myself busy that night by running a few séances in the tea room! Was this what Dad had meant in the dream? He came through immediately as the first 'guest' at the séance, spelling out his name on my angel board as I sat round the table with a selection of the 'ghost hunter' guests. Dad, 'RON', introduced himself as the 'host' from the spirit world.

Next the lights flickered above the table and the spirit board message spelled out ERIC. My late Uncle Eric was in charge of flickering the lights to indicate a new spirit guest was being introduced to the table. What fun! Each time a loved one appeared, Eric made the lights flicker and Dad spelled out the name for them. What a great team.

I'm sure the living visitors to the castle that night had expected a spooky evening … they were at the castle for a ghost hunt, after all. But this wasn't spooky … not this bit, anyway. One by one Dad introduced family members for those present. He was helping loved ones to spell out their names on the board … my angel board! The ghosts of Tutbury Castle never got the opportunity to communicate at all!

The messages were extraordinary. Full names were spelled out, the numbers of children, details of where people had lived and so on. Many guests asked questions and the answers were spelled out clearly, too … sometimes when the intended recipient wasn't even touching the pointer on the table.

One or two people cried – in happiness. The messages were so clear. I imagine it's a shock to discover that the afterlife is a real place and our loved ones are well and 'texting' loving messages from heaven. Spirit boards can provide some of the clearest evidence I have ever seen … as long as they are used safely, with psychic protection and by an experienced medium.

The Castle tea room was crowded with people: people from this side of life and people from the other side. Guests took it in turn to sit at the table. Many guests made contact with their loved ones that night, and it was as much a surprise to me as it was to them.

I remembered Dad's message in the 'bus visitation' dream. He was helping me to pass on messages from the other side, just as he'd promised. Dad had died but he was here right now – very much still at work.

Chapter 2

Mystic Dad

'Every man contemplates an angel in his future self.'
Ralph Waldo Emerson

WORKING WITH THE ANGELS

Dad lets me know that he is around by constantly showing me signs. Yesterday I was working on my computer when the batteries failed in my computer mouse. I couldn't get anything to work. What was interesting is the batteries had recently been changed. OK, so perhaps it was a coincidence … I'll accept that – but then, at almost the same moment, my CD player halted in mid-song. The music just stopped playing for no reason, yet no other electrical items were affected during this time … only these two (out of many other electrical items in my office). Sounds spooky, right? But surprisingly it wasn't too scary.

So let's say that one interruption of energy (electricity) is normal, twice is unusual – but what happened next makes it a 'sign', I think. I decided to go out in the car for a while with Mum, and left the house ten minutes later. Now, my car doesn't have autolock for the doors, but no sooner had I sat in the car than the doors locked … then just as quickly unlocked again! Come on … three things in the space of a few minutes is weird, right? Yes, I believe it was Dad! Sometimes when I'm in the car talking about him the windscreen wipers start up on their own, too. He has so many tricks up his sleeve, but the signs are usually about meaningful coincidences (synchronicity), and include several things happening in one go.

Since Dad passed away my own guardian angel (my spirit guide) has retreated into the background a little. I guess because Dad is a more familiar energy, he is easier for me to converse with.

One day I was communicating on the angel board and Dad confirmed my thoughts.

'You now have three guardian angels working with you,' he spelled out. Intrigued, I asked him if he had names for these exalted beings.

'Yes,' he explained. 'Dad … Jack … and Eric!'

'What?????' I laughed. 'You're not angels!' But I was comforted to know they were close. Not angels in the traditional sense, but my personal angels! Dad, father-in-law and uncle – my very own three wise men!

THE YOUTH CANCER TRUST

That June I was stunned to be invited to become a patron of the Youth Cancer Trust. Dad had had cancer, and I realized how important it was to support cancer charities of all sorts.

The Youth Cancer Trust was set up to provide holidays in sunny Bournemouth for young people suffering from cancer and malignant diseases. Although Bournemouth is a long way from where I live, I was thrilled to be asked to help and knew immediately that I could mention the charity in many of the features and magazine articles that I write. Promotion … I was good at that!

EXPERIENCING THE SIXTH SENSE WITH TV PSYCHICS

I get asked to attend a lot of events as a guest speaker/ workshop tutor, but hands down the most fun is the local event, 'Experience the Sixth Sense', organized by a local ghost-hunting group called 'Swadlincote Paranormal'. The first year was over-subscribed fourfold, and I'm not surprised. The local group gather together a very large group of well-known TV psychics and mediums … and me (being a local girl)!

I rarely get to have my family along to events, so it's always special when I do. These local events mean the family can support me. We run a big book stall and I get the opportunity to meet fans and sign books. This year I bumped into *Most Haunted* guest mediums David Wells, Phil Whyman, Ian Lawman and Barrie John, and *Ghost Detectives'* Richard Felix. Also at the event were Angela McGhee (author of *Angela's Angels* and guest star of Living TV's *Psychic Investigators*) and Mark Webb (from *Haunted Homes* and *I'm Famous and Frightened*). I have worked with many of these people before, so we are like old friends now. The first time I met Richard Felix I was interviewing him for a magazine and my husband and I took him for lunch. Once he and David Wells sneaked us into the live audience of *Most Haunted* at Derby! It was fun when friends called me on my mobile later to tell me they'd spotted us in the audience! David is also an old friend.

Sister Debbie was on hand to take loads of photographs and, like many fans, was fascinated with Richard Felix's famous long black 'Batman' leather coat. As soon as Richard popped out of the green room for just a moment Debbie kidnapped the coat and tried it on! (I have photographic evidence at my website www.JackyNewcomb.com.) Shhh, don't tell Richard!

Ghost hunters are fascinated with orbs – balls of light which show up on photographs. Some believe they are simply specks of dust, water vapour or insects, yet others believe they are spirits or angels (more of this later). Debbie took several photographs of Barrie, Richard and me as we took to the stage together. Strangely, afterwards we discovered a couple of orbs on one of the photos. Maybe someone was up on the stage helping us … or perhaps it was Dad again. (He does get the 'blame' for everything now!)

The most famous 'person' at the event was a Dalek from the TV show *Dr Who*! Barrie and I posed for a photograph with the deadly Dalek, who sprayed his 'terrifying' smoke into the camera. As soon as we had posed for this we ran for it (wouldn't you be scared? OK, so it wasn't real, but just to be on the safe side, you understand …). When we were children we always used to hide behind the sofa when the Daleks came on TV! Ha! Ha!

BIGGEST FAN

On Mum's birthday, her first as a widow, I popped round to her apartment to show her the second Japanese edition of one of my books which had arrived that morning. It was the translated version of my book *Angels Watching Over Me* with my photo on the jacket. I am always excited when a new book drops on the doormat. It reminded me of how Dad collected copies of everything that I ever did … every book, magazine article and every photo of me standing next to a celebrity.

He was so proud, like most dads, and was my biggest fan. These are the things that we miss sharing when we lose a loved one, but for me the sadness has not been what it might. Dad's regular dream-visits keep him very much alive in my life.

In October I was invited to attend the SC Awards on the south coast of England because I had been nominated for the award for Best Author. These fun nights are organized to recognize people who work in the spiritual and holistic field. It's like our Oscars!

I was very excited to attend, as I had been lucky enough to win the award for best author the year before. My husband John and my sister Debbie sat with me and our friends the medium Barrie John and his manager and business partner Jay. I felt that Dad was also right at our table. He would have been thrilled to have known that I was nominated again … but of course he did know!

You never want to plan a speech ahead of time – it's a sort of jinx – but I figured that if I won again I would thank Dad for his support and dedicate the award to him! But when my name was called as the winner I was stunned. To be honest, I hadn't really been paying attention!

Walking up to the stage, all I could concentrate on was my slippery shoes … imagine the embarrassment of falling over! I was wearing a full-length purple sequined gown and the presenter, BBC broadcast journalist Brian Smith, was teasing me about it: 'Look at that dress, wow, come on girl, work it … work it … ' I giggled as I wiggled my way up to the stage (without falling off my heels) but once

I got up there I completely forgot what I was going to say … hysterical! So I confidently waffled for a few moments and wiggled back off the stage. Walking back to my seat I found a beautiful white feather stuck to the carpet – a gift from Dad, maybe, or the angels? Or was someone wearing a feather boa?

One of the organizers come up to the table and asked me if I would present the award for 'Most Popular Spiritual Male'. Of course I was delighted to be up on the stage again, and this time the winner was my dear friend Barrie. He told me afterwards that he knew he had won because my face had completely given it away. As I opened the envelope and paused for effect … apparently I looked right at him! (Doh!)

Another friend, *Most Haunted*'s David Wells, had also been nominated for an award but because of work commitments abroad he was unable to attend that evening. He'd contacted me earlier and asked me to collect his award if he won, so I had three trips to the stage altogether. Barrie also collected an award on behalf of a friend, so we had quite a collection of awards on the table. Debbie had enormous fun later in the evening posing with all the awards gathered around her.

We had a wonderful time and it reminded me of a strange premonition someone told me about, years ago – a psychic (I didn't know her) emailed me and told me that she could see me standing on a stage collecting an award; she also predicted that I would be on the cover of a magazine. In her vision I had blonde hair. I'd laughed at the time because my hair is naturally brown (shhh, our little secret). I told her there was no way I would ever colour my hair … blonde.

Several years later here I was, blonde for the second year running and collecting an award … and, yes, I'd been on the cover of a magazine, too. I love it when a happy premonition comes true!

DAD VISITS DEBBIE

'Did I tell you Dad visited me a couple of nights ago?' my sister ventured.

'No. There are so many visits now we often forget to share them with the rest of the family … we mustn't get complacent! What happened?'

' … More of the usual. He and Eric both appeared.'

'Yes?'

'It was so funny, Jacky. They were both lying back with their hands behind their heads; they looked like they were lying on sun-loungers but they were floating on clouds!'

'You're kidding, right?'

'No, seriously! They were both laughing their heads off, as usual. Then Dad gave me a hug and they were on their way. I think they were just passing through … .'

'That's so funny! I did a workshop recently and I took

the delegates through a guided meditation – I had them floating on clouds. Did I tell you?'

'No, you never mentioned it.'

'Well, it seems like two "fellows" were snooping in on my workshop and making fun of me!' We both giggled. Dad and Uncle Eric are so funny … 'dead funny', Dad would say!

MUM HAS A HEART ATTACK

'Hi, Dad, is something the matter?' I was asleep but Dad was visiting again from the afterlife. He had a serious look on his face. He was standing at the top of a hospital bed, and I seemed to be sitting at the bottom of the bed on a chair. Mum was lying in the bed.

Why was Dad showing me this vision of Mum in a hospital bed? Dad had been ill for years before he'd passed over. He'd had a stomach ulcer, stroke, car accidents, brain tumour … you name it. We'd spent years sitting at Dad's hospital bedside, but Mum was never ill. Why was Mum in the hospital now? What was Dad trying to tell me?

'Don't worry,' he reassured me. 'No matter what the doctors say, Mum is going to be just fine. She has many, many years to live.' Scarily, he actually gave me a 'time line' as to when this might be – but luckily it was a very long way off in the future!

The next morning I told Mum about my dream

experience (I didn't tell her that Dad had predicted the date when she might actually die … far into the distant future! Who wants to know that?)

Mum laughed when I told her; we both did. This couldn't be right, surely? But several days later Mum's heart rhythm was abnormal. The doctor rushed her into hospital – she was having a heart attack!

We were used to the 'drill', as we'd done this so many times with Dad and knew the hospital emergency department very well.

Mum had popped to the doctor's surgery with no handbag, no phone and without informing any of us that she was going. The doctor phoned for the ambulance right away and she was rushed right in … she hadn't even locked her door!

My sisters and I all sat on her bed at the hospital. We looked terrified and ill, Mum looked great! It was such a bizarre experience that I actually took a photograph of her in the hospital. She'd had a heart attack – how could she look so well?

We discussed my vision of a few nights earlier and knew that Dad was taking care of Mum. At first doctors were concerned, but after many tests decided she could go home … the very next morning, accompanied by a very large bag of new pills.

Just as Dad had predicted in the dream, Mum was perfectly fine. In fact, a few days later we all visited the

Health and Healing Festival in Buxton, Derbyshire. I took another photograph of Mum. She was wearing a pretty pink top and her face just glowed. It was the nicest photograph I had ever seen of her and she had the most amazing inner light about her. Now tell me that Dad and the gang weren't working on healing her from the inside out!

GLORIA HUNNIFORD, CLIFF RICHARD ... AND FAITH BROWN

'You're going to meet Gloria Hunniford and Cliff Richard!' I randomly said to Mum one day, long before Dad passed over. It was one of those strange premonitions I get from time to time.

'What about me?' Dad called out from the lounge, and we all laughed.

'Ohh, lovely,' said Mum in a slightly sarcastic way. (I'm sure she thinks I'm nuts!)

Actually I'd worked with TV presenter and broadcaster Gloria previously. We both made an appearance on the TV show *This Morning* as guests of Fern Britton and Phillip Schofield. The topic was angels, and Gloria is a big fan too!

Gloria was delightful and very generous with her time. We had nearly an hour together before appearing on the show, and she talked lovingly about her daughter, the late TV presenter Caron Keating.

Gloria and her sons had set up a website in Caron's name: http://www.caronkeating.org/. The organization raises funds for cancer charities and had previously donated a large sum of money to the Youth Cancer Trust (the charity of which I am a patron).

Twelve months after my strange premonition, not all that long after Dad passed and just two months after Mum's heart attack, I received an invitation. It was a ticket to the Caron Keating Ball, an event organized by a lovely woman called Joy Passman, and the theme of the evening was to celebrate singer Cliff Richard's 50th anniversary in show business.

I couldn't believe it! This must be what I'd seen in my premonition! It was the perfect opportunity for Mum to meet Cliff and Gloria – I couldn't have planned it better myself.

Of course I immediately suggested that Mum come, too, and husband John drove Mum, sister Debbie and me to the event. It was a magical evening, and towards the end of the night Sir Cliff Richard arrived with his close friend Gloria Hunniford. Cliff sang a special song, 'Miss You Nights', in honour of his late friend Caron. It was mind-blowing as we all crowded round him on the dance floor. The evening was as intimate as sitting in my living room at home, and I couldn't believe I'd been lucky enough to have been invited.

Faith Brown, the impressionist, singer and actress, was in attendance to run the auction on the night. She made thousands of pounds for the charity by auctioning off Cliff Richard memorabilia. Faith posed for hours with guests and was a real star. What a lovely woman!

Debbie was armed with her camera and was my 'official' photographer on the night. Faith suggested a fun pose where she and I stood back to back. Now Faith is well known for her 'ample' bosoms, and so the photograph was hilarious! Afterwards I discovered a similar photograph that she'd posed for with model Jordan (Katie Price) – but I think Jordan and Faith were a better match in size! Our photograph was totally unbalanced and much giggling ensued.

Debbie was on a mission to get a photograph of Mum and me with Cliff and Gloria, and using the full force of her connections managed to manipulate us into the VIP room. Tragically just as we squeezed in the room they announced that Cliff had to leave … what, no photo? Nooooo!

Everything had transpired to get us to this event, so we weren't going to give up that easily. Quick as a flash I gave Mum a shove next to Cliff and I stood next to Gloria. 'Smile, everyone!' I yelled gleefully and Debbie managed to take a single shot. It was perfect. Mum and I look like good friends of Cliff and Gloria in the photograph … but of course we had never even met Cliff before! Mum was thrilled with the shot as she'd been a big fan of Cliff Richard for years. She looked up at him and in a small voice said, 'Thanks for coming!' Bless her!

A premonition which came true, and now Mum had the photograph to prove it. I was able to use it (with permission) in several magazine articles where I was able to mention the Caron Keating Foundation (please support them if you can). Success … another premonition comes true! (Pictures at my website: www.JackyNewcomb.com)

A RED ROSE

Twelve months after his passing we took Dad's ashes to be sprinkled under a tree at a lake in our village. John and I had recently celebrated our 25th wedding anniversary and the house was full of flowers. Just as I left the house, the roses caught my eye, so I plucked a single stemmed red rose to give to Mum.

We collected Mum and the ashes in the car, and the rest of the family followed behind us. When we got to the lake Mum turned round and said, 'Oh, I meant to ask you if I could have one of your roses so I could throw it onto the water after we sprinkled the ashes.' But of course I had already brought a rose for her … prompted by Dad, no doubt, and it was hidden in the boot of the car!

Mum immediately told me a funny story. When he used to go to his lodge meetings Dad would bring Mum home a single red rose. He always arrived home late and Mum would be in bed, so he used to carry the rose to her in his teeth!

The ashes were in a tall jar. It was heavy and not what I had expected at all. Mum had brought along some small tiny-headed daffodil bulbs (narcissi) and we decided to plant the bulbs under a nearby tree next to the lake. Strangely, when we chose the ideal tree we noticed a perfect 'plant-sized' hole in the ground, almost as if it had been dug for the purpose! My friend Wendy teased me that we blocked up some poor rabbit's home with our flower bulbs, but I promise we didn't.

I'd brought along a plastic spoon so we could each scoop some of the ashes onto the flowering bulbs (as well as the lake). I thought it would be a symbol of new and old life – but by the time several of us had scooped ash onto the plant the plastic spoon broke in half! You never know whether to laugh or cry when these things happen, but we all laughed. It was probably another heavenly trick anyway!

MUM MEETS TV'S NICK OWEN

I've previously done some work with my local St Giles Hospice, so when I discovered that TV newsreader and anchorman Nick Owen was appearing at a lunch to raise funds for the Hospice, I contacted Mum. Mum was already well known for her Cliff Richard photograph, and this would be a fun opportunity of her adding to her collection of 'celebrity photographs'.

Nick is a friend of my agent and her partner, and I was looking forward to meeting him personally. Nick gave a hysterical after-lunch talk, sharing fun stories about his TV friends, and I realized how important this type of event has become in fundraising. He was giving me some fundraising ideas of my own!

Mum and I chatted to Nick for ages and after the event he rushed on back to work. He was appearing on TV later in the afternoon and still had to drive back to the studio. These celebrities are very hard-working people indeed, and of course ... Mum and I got our photograph with the lovely Nick!

It had been a sad year with losing Dad, but these events were a welcome distraction.

'Dad' Sends a Christmas Gift

At Christmas a friend of Dad's popped round to bring Mum a bunch of yellow roses. This dear man had no idea that his unexpected gift had so much meaning for Mum. Mum and Dad chose yellow roses for their wedding 53 years previously, and Dad often bought Mum yellow roses as gifts over the years.

Perhaps Dad influenced his friend's choice of gift, sending them from the flower shop in heaven.

RADIO INTERVIEWS

I've always done a lot of radio interviews, and this year has been no exception. I have several favourites whom I have been interviewed by over and over again, including Talk Sport Radio's *The Unexplained* with Howard Hughes and presenter Keith Middleton. We always have such a laugh on air.

Another favourite is Philip Solomon; he has interviewed many famous names and is a medium himself. I always give out my personal mobile number to the presenters when booking to do a radio show because I have a 'paranoid' fear of forgetting I'm appearing on the show – with good reason: embarrassingly, I have forgotten in the past.

The night I was due to go on Philip's show I had a couple of hours to spare and decided to visit Mum for an hour. We were drinking coffee in the residents' lounge in her beautiful apartment building when my mobile rang ... you guessed it, I'd forgotten the show. I offered to race round the corner to my house but Philip was happy enough to chat to me on the mobile phone. I did the whole interview while residents popped in and out of the restaurant and, you know what? No one even noticed! Hysterical!

Another night I did an interview with the online radio station 'White Noise'. It was a fun show but on several occasions the sound completely disappeared and at one point they had to 'jump start' the show again. This often happens to me when I'm on air – it's like 'spirit interference' on the airways! I imagine that my guides and angels tune in, and all that static messes things up a bit.

Memory of a Phone-in Show That Never Happened!

Writing this story up reminded me of something else that happened once. Years ago I was given the opportunity of appearing on a TV programme which was recorded in London. The show was a phone-in psychic programme, but when I got to the studio I was amazed to discover that the studio was also used to record the evening 'lady-chat' lines! The studio was full of beds and photographs of scantily-clad ladies! I'm not easily shockable but this was very funny!

I was amazed that my 'angel guides' had led me to the show, because normally they would have steered me away from something like this. Then, weirdly, there was a 'technical' problem and the show was unable to go out that day! The show didn't even start – and I never got to record a single word.

Maybe the blend of energies wasn't right for the 'angel lady', but John and I had a good laugh about it on the drive home!

* * * *

It's been a funny old year. Topics which I write about and research all the time have now become part of my everyday life: Dad has been appearing in dream-visitations (real visits from his spirit while my body was asleep) every week. All in all, Dad has visited around 20 other family members and friends (some of whom knew nothing about the phenomenon and just reported 'strange and extraordinarily real' dreams.)

I've known for many years that the afterlife is a genuine place (space) and now I have a direct line to the afterlife! I'm convinced that over the next few years Dad (and the 'angels') will be helping with my research from this side of life. I can't wait to find out what happens next!

In the meantime, I hope you enjoy the many special stories and letters that I've received over the last year, and that you learn just a little bit more about the other realms as a result.

Part II

Chapter 3

Your Guardian Angel Questions

'It is not because angels are holier than men or devils that makes them angels, but because they do not expect holiness from one another, but from God alone.'
William Blake

What is an angel? Can my grandma be my angel? This and many more are regular questions in my postbag. We all like to feel secure and safe, and your angel can seem like a big, warm, fluffy blanket at times. The musician and TV presenter Myleene Klass has told me that her guardian angel feels like her mum, and I think she's right. Mums give unconditional love, and so do our guardian angels.

I have edited the letters that follow very lightly and mainly only for spelling. In some cases I have taken out irrelevant or unrelated information, but that's about all. I've tried to distribute the information evenly in each chapter, so that if you have a question of your own on a specific topic you should be able to find what you are looking for.

Some questions are very short and some are … well, very long. Rather than shorten the longer questions I thought you might like the opportunity to read in a little more detail about the real lives and experiences behind them.

WHAT ARE ANGELS?

Let's start at the very beginning, then. One of my most-asked questions of all time!

Dear Jacky
This may sound a stupid question and I know you probably get asked this all the time, but what exactly are angels, and how will I know when I've met one?
Ryan, Canada

Dear Ryan
No question is ever stupid if you don't know the answer! The world 'angel' means messenger, or 'light being', and, unlike humans, they were created to serve God. Angels were formed without 'free will' (freedom of choice) unlike humankind … we are given freedom of choice (the only limitations are legal ones within each country or limits of our physical bodies or of our own making).

Angels appear to people in many different ways. Some see them as human-like beings and others as figures with large white wings or surrounded by a bright white light. I know that some people see them as a pure light-energy, and yet others see angels as twinkling lights.

Angels appear to people in dreams and visions, and angels can sometimes seem so like human souls that they can be momentarily confused with human beings … especially when they are seen out and about. It's only afterwards that people say that the 'person' who stopped to help them, ' … wore strange clothes', or ' … had the most amazing blonde hair and piercing blue eyes' and so on.

When you ask someone how they knew for sure that they encountered a real angel, that person has a deep inner knowing, often accompanied by a powerful feeling of love or peace afterwards. When you meet an angel you 'just know', and if it ever happens to you, then I'm sure that you will know, too.
Jacky

DO WE ALL HAVE ANGELS?

As human souls we like to feel we are not alone in the universe. I firmly believe that we do have our own protectors and guardians. Here is one of the many letters I have received on the subject.

Dear Jacky
I am feeling really low at the moment and I don't know which way my life is heading. They say everyone has an angel. I would like to know, do I have one?
Karen, England

Hi there, Karen
We ALL have guardian angels and also spirit guides working with us all the time. Angels are beings of pure light whose jobs range from messenger to protector. Never feel you are abandoned, because you're not. Their help and support are there when you need them.

According to Schott's *Almanac of Belief*, 26 per cent of men believe in guardian angels, while 50 per cent of women are believers. I know those numbers will just grow and grow. Never fear, you do have a guardian angel by your side.
Jacky

I also directed Karen to some of the communication ideas that I have in my books, *A Little Angel Love* and *An Angel Saved My Life* (like Karen, you can also visit my website for more information: www.AngelLady.co.uk).

Communicating with your own angels is a very personal thing. Each of us works in different ways in our normal day-to-day lives, and our angels recognize this fact. Over time we can build a relationship with our celestial advisors in a way that feels right to us. Are you someone who works with feelings or are you more visual? Your angel will know.

CAN OUR RELATIVES AND LOVED ONES ON THE OTHER SIDE BE OUR GUARDIAN ANGELS?

Dear Angel Lady
We lost my dear mother-in-law last year and she was only 50 years old. Recently my children have been talking about her being around them like a guardian angel. Is this possible?
Lorraine, Wales

Hi Lorraine
Yes, it is possible. They aren't real angels as such (in the traditional meaning of the word angel), but they are watching over you. Children are very open to this experience, and very accepting of love continuing from the other side.

My own relatives are around a lot (and I have experienced much personal proof from them that they are really with me). They are particularly aware of important occasions in our lives like weddings, birthdays and family get-togethers, and are heard and felt more at these times.
Jacky

Hi Jacky

Would you be able to tell me if my angel could be my mum?

Thank you.

Kerry, USA

Hi Kerry

Although our relatives are NOT real angels, they still help us in an 'angelic' way from the other side, which is why people often say that passed-over relatives are 'guardian angels' (purely an affectionate term).

Although their powers are limited they can sometimes intervene and give us helpful thoughts, ideas and information. Relatives on the other side have even been known to jump in with a bit of life-saving information, too. They love us, just as they always did, and if they can help out, you bet they're going to try.

Jacky

ANGELS HELPING US

It is the angels' greatest pleasure, in fact it is one of their reasons for 'being', to help us. What we have to remember, though, is to ask the angels for their help. Don't forget that little rule we talked about: humans are born with free will and the angels (and other spiritual beings) are not allowed to interfere with our life plan. They can help us to move through our lessons, though, and do this in many different ways.

Have you ever heard of the saying 'Beware of entertaining angels unawares'? I receive a lot of letters from people who believe that angels have appeared to them. Are these angels appearing in human form, or are they just kindly humans 'being angelic' in nature? What do you think?

Dear Angel Lady

Six years ago I was a single parent, waitressing for a living and generally having a very hard time. We had to move to a new area and I didn't know a soul; I was at the lowest I think I could ever be.

I had a clapped-out old car and advertised to sell it for £50 because I could no longer run it. A couple came to look at it. They were dressed in bright rainbow-coloured jumpers! They gave me £75 for the car. Following on from that day, every Friday I came home from work to find a bag of groceries from them on my doorstep. This went on for some time, and it was always the nice things that you don't normally get when you're hard up, like nice coffees and chocolates.

After I'd managed to get my life on track I started to think about the possibility of these two being

angels, and now I'm sure they were. I wonder if they are my permanent angels or just happened to be there at the time. I'd be interested to know. Maybe they were just very nice people. I'd love to know what you think about this.
Anne, England

Hello, Anne
Thank you for writing to me. What a wonderful story! Angels can appear to us in the guise of humans, and this happens a lot. Often they stand out (although I'm sure they do not mean to) – they regularly have blonde hair, bright blue eyes and are very tall. Sometimes they appear to wear clothing which seems out of place, or clothing which is from an earlier period in time or doesn't go together (trainers and pearls, for example).

I also think that there are 'Earth angels': humans whose only role is to help others in need. We all find ourselves doing 'angel work' from time to time. Imagine if you could afford to be able to do what these people did for you and go out and help others! I bet they had pleasure for years, knowing they could help you in this way.

I always feel there is a golden rule to these things, and if and when it's possible we should take the opportunity to be Earth angels, too, to do something nice for someone who does not know you are doing it ... one of life's greatest pleasures.

Were they 'real' angels or human angels? I'm not sure – perhaps it doesn't matter.

Jacky

ANGELS AND GOD

I believe we are all watched over and protected from the other side. Our religious beliefs or lack of them does not seem to affect the help we receive in any way.

We all experience angels in ways that are perfect for us. Don't get too bogged down about what you don't believe or find difficult to include in your life. Follow what feels right for you at this moment in time and see how things develop. There are so many things in heaven and Earth that we don't understand. If these feelings and experiences are comforting and helpful, then just go with the flow. Enjoy it.

Many people want to work with angels, and write to ask if their religious beliefs will hinder or forbid them from doing so. I suggest we all look within for the answer. People of all religious backgrounds, and those with no belief in God, write to tell me they believe in angels … go figure! Angels are mentioned in almost every religion, and even people who have no religious beliefs still believe in angels!

I remember when I was at school, my religious education teacher sent for my parents. He demanded that they come and visit, as he had something he urgently wanted to discuss with them. Young Jacky had said that she didn't believe in God! Imagine!

I think I didn't know what God was, and with lack of any 'proof' in my life I decided to 'opt out' of believing in a supreme creator. It certainly caused a bit of a stir at the time, which seems strange now as I have a very strong faith. It doesn't matter where faith begins … it has to start somewhere! I call myself 'spiritual' ... and yes, I believe in God.

Hi Jacky

As I do not believe in a 'god' – is it still possible to work with angels?

Many thanks.

Jenny, Scotland

Hello, Jenny

Angels are said to be created by God and they form part of many religions but are not 'tied' to any religion.

Some people call psychic ability 'natural intuition', others call the help of guardian angels 'instinct' and so on. 'God' is thought of in different ways by different people, too. Maybe you don't believe in a supreme creator, but does a single energy or creative source feel right to you?

Whatever your beliefs, angels are ready, willing and able to work with us all, so follow your own instincts and do what works best for you. Remember, if you want to work with the angels, then they will definitely want to work with you!

You will find your own way through … trust your own thoughts and feelings on the subject.

Jacky

ANGEL NAMES

It surprises me how much information we pick up from our angels and spirit guides, including their names. Actually our angels and guides do not mind what we call them, so if a name does come to you and you feel comfortable with that name, then my advice is to use it if you want. Here is a letter on that very subject.

Dear Jacky

I saw your article in *Woman's Own* a few weeks back. I very much believe in the power of angels, but have never been able to find the name of my guardian angel. I have a lovely angel statue in my room, called Hope. She is carrying a basket of roses (it puts me in mind of an early saint called Dorothea. There is a delightful story about her and roses). Could I use that name for my own guardian angel?

Also, do you know of any other way of being able to come to terms with people (both friends and in other types of situations) who have hurt you very deeply in the past? One way I read about is to write to your guardian angel about how you feel (which has worked in some cases).

I hope you can be of help. Thanks.

G. L., Ireland

Hello

Yes, definitely use the name Dorothea. In fact, as soon as I read the name it felt right. I actually feel that this is the name of your spiritual guide rather than a guardian angel, and that you have picked up the name intuitively; this may be the reason you feel so connected to it.

Dealing with past hurt is difficult. Writing to the other person's angels might work, as long as your request is sent with love and understanding. Remember, we can't interfere with someone else's free will (even if they are mean).

Writing to your own angels can be a much better way of dealing with the situation. It's a safe way to vent your initial anger, and you can ask your own guardian angels to help you to deal with your feelings over the hurt.

I have lots more information about how to work with your angels in my book, *An Angel Treasury*, or visit my website for some more ideas there.
Jacky

US HELPING ANGELS

Helping the angels is something that people rarely ask me about ... surprisingly. Mostly people want to know how the angels can help them, so this was a rare letter indeed. But I've included it here as I felt it followed on beautifully from the previous one.

Dear Jacky
I was just wondering how to say 'Thank you' and show appreciation to my angels for all of the wonderful things they do for me. Is there anything they want us to do for them?
Many thanks.
Nicole, Wales

Hello, Nicole
Indeed there is, and angels will often inspire us to assist others in need. There are opportunities to help people every single day. I would suggest starting with your own family.

- When people want (or need) to talk, try and stop what you are doing and give them a little time. Your efforts will mean such a lot.
- A simple thing like smiling at a stranger is so easy.
- How about striking up a conversation with someone when you are standing together at the bus stop, train station ... or sitting in a hot tub at your local spa!
- Can you pick up a neighbour's shopping when he is ill; watch over a friend's child when she is late home from work or help out your pregnant sister by running the vacuum cleaner round the living room? Simple things mean a lot.

Look out for your own ways of helping people. Think of your activities as being like a 'Secret Santa'. Sometimes it's even more fun to do acts of kindness anonymously. It doesn't matter how you help, just do something ... and have fun.

Angel blessings.

Jacky

When you've helped the angels you feel wonderful inside. If you feel down and depressed in your own life, I promise you will feel better by helping someone else. That inner glow is really something to treasure.

SEEING ANGELS

People write to me in great distress because they are wanting their angels to contact them. They read about dramatic angel experiences and want something similar for themselves.

Angels work in my life every day. I've heard angel music, felt their presence and even heard whispers of wisdom and guidance, but I rarely see them. Seeing angels is probably the most unlikely way to experience angels in your life, but it does leave people disappointed when they don't experience what they expect (or hope for).

Angels take part in most people's lives by helping us to make changes and bring 'coincidences' to assist us in moving forward and growing in our lives through experience. In other words, angels help us to help ourselves.

If we ask angels for help, they do hear us. Do you really want an angel taller than your house to appear before you? You may think you'd like this to happen, but actually you probably don't really!

Ask angels for help and it arrives – but not always in the way that you expect! Look out for signs that bring you the assistance you need. Have you told your angels you are lonely? Then watch out for an old friend to call you out of the blue. Do you need a new job? Expect to bump into someone who is looking for an employee just like you. Keep talking to people about what is going on in your life and see what happens. Remember that we have to create the magic in our own lives and the angels just help us along – they don't live our lives for us, and we wouldn't want them to. We are the co-creators of our world.

THE ANGELS OF GRIEF

Losing a loved one left this woman in a great deal of distress and looking for comfort and reassurance from her angels.

Dear Angel Lady

At the end of March my father passed away. I nursed him for the last few weeks of his life, which was very distressing for me. Since his passing I have suffered ill health both physically and mentally.

I have always believed in angels and the afterlife. I began to read a lot more about this type of thing since Dad's passing and one day I was watching a television programme about a woman who had been going through a particularly bad time. She said that she didn't really believe in the afterlife or angels, and so she shouted out for proof because she was desperate. To her amazement she said that an angel walked into the room. The angel sat her down and showed her that her future was 'rosy', and the woman said that she was overwhelmed by the experience and that she would never doubt again.

I now have a question for you in the hope that you can help: I have asked my guardian angel to come to me many, many times in order to reassure me that I will be OK. Often during this difficult time I have just wanted to curl up and die. Dad was a huge part of my life, we were very close. My guardian angel has never come and this has only added to my grief.

So my question is: why do guardian angels appear to some and not others? Is there anything in particular that I can do to summon my guardian angel to come, because the way I feel right now I would welcome any intervention into my life just to give me some reassurance.

Thank you for your time.

Rachel, England

Dear Rachel

I am so sorry for your loss. The death of a loved one can be a devastating experience, and physical symptoms following loss are very common.

This woman's story is fairly rare and usually happens when people are in danger or deep distress (although not always). This particular experience happened to a woman who is now a best-selling angel author herself. It seems likely that the reason she saw an angel in this way (even though it is difficult for angels to appear like that) was because her story was part of her life mission … to share her experience and teach others.

People do have dramatic angel encounters, but for most people their experiences are far more subtle. Mostly angels do not make dramatic appearances because it is pretty terrifying. Remember the shepherds in the Bible? The poor shepherds were terrified when the angels appeared to them – it doesn't say they were excited! The angels announced themselves with the words, 'Do not be afraid!'

Your angels will know that you want them to be a part of your life, but you are vulnerable right now. You may be missing their subtle signs. Sometimes we are so busy waiting and looking for something spectacular that we miss the obvious smaller connections.

These simple connections might include some of the following:

- Finding white feathers in unusual places or just when you ask for a sign.
- Seeing words in car number plates or messages in posters – your angels guide you to see the words you need to read.
- The words of a book stand out to you … words that you need to hear or that give you the answer to a question you have asked.

- You feel guided to do something or go somewhere. That subtle sense which leads you in the direction of help from human sources.
- You sense that you are not alone, or feel a loving touch on your hand or perhaps your shoulder.
- You receive messages in dreams, or wake up with the answer clearly in your mind.

Be nice to yourself. Your dad and your angels are waiting to communicate when your heart is ready.
Jacky x

THE RIGHT ANGEL FOR THE JOB

There are as many angels are there are people – lots more, actually – and each angel has a specific task and role. There are several angels that help children.

Hi Jacky
I wonder if you could let me know which angel to speak to in order for my children to benefit?
Thank you.
Karla, USA

Hi Karla
Archangel Michael offers protection; Archangel Gabriel helps with communication and adoption! Child healing would be Ariel, and

childbirth Gabriel again. Confidence is Zadkiel; Raguel helps to resolve conflicts, and freedom of thought would be Jophiel.

Try Sariel for hygiene problems, Zadkiel for memory (helpful for homework). Problem solving would be Archangel Uriel. Sariel works with the spirit of the child and Archangel Sandalphon is the angel in charge of unborn babies.

Gabriel is seen as a female angel in some religions and therefore the one most used for children. A long answer to a short question!

I hope this helps, but don't worry too much about remembering all of this. Just ask, 'Please send the right angel for the job' and know that it is done, or ask for help from the child's own guardian angel (or the child can ask for himself, if he is old enough).
Jacky

ANGELS AND HEALING

I receive some wonderful stories of angels helping with healing. Sometimes the stories can be about something simple, where the writer has felt an angel presence; at other times the story is more spectacular, as this letter demonstrates.

Dear Angel Lady

I have always loved my angels and I know they are always with me.

Last April, Good Friday to be exact, I had an emergency operation on my back. Before the operation the surgeons told me I probably would not walk again and I would be doubly incontinent. I was terrified and I knew in my heart I was finished with nursing (I had been a nursing assistant for 26 years). My whole world was crashing down around me, so the surgeon left me with my own thoughts.

I said to my angels (I feel their names are Kay and Olivia), 'Right, you heard the man; please take this fear from me.' In a matter of seconds the fear had left me and I was at peace with the world.

At 2 o'clock in the morning, without any pre-med, I was wheeled away to the theatre. I was talking away to the nurses and I was so relaxed. Anyway, two of my discs had collapsed, so the surgeon removed the discs and replaced them with bones from my hips. It was a long and delicate operation.

After the operation I was put into the recovery room and I felt someone stroking my arm and my hair. I knew it was not my husband or my family as they didn't know I'd had my operation. I opened my eyes for a minute and saw one of my angels, and she smiled and told me all would be well.

Then I fell asleep again, and as I was coming round I felt a tingle from my toes right up my legs; I knew then I would have a hard road in front of me, but would come through it. I had to wear a body brace for six months, but with the love of my husband and family I can walk again. I am now back at work (not as a nurse but as a ward clerk).

I thank God and my angels every day, and I still talk to my angels all the time.

Marion, England

Dear Marion

Thank you for sharing your wonderful and uplifting story. I am sure that many people will be comforted by reading it.

Jacky

People on the edge of consciousness can sometimes see angels. Being in an altered state of consciousness (like meditating or dreaming, for example) does help. At that time we are closer to the angels' 'vibration', meeting them in the middle somewhat (when we are unconscious our vibrational level is raised; the angels lower their vibration to meet it). Of course, becoming unconscious is not something we choose to do on purpose, but you can certainly meditate to bring about a faster vibration.

By clearing and relaxing our mind and body we leave a little space for the angels to communicate … to be able to reach in. Many have success using this method to reach out to those on the higher realms.

A guided meditation (usually a voice talking you through a 'journey' or visualization, to meet with your angel) is fun. Sometimes this is done with background music and sometimes not. I have created several guided meditation CDs (reveries), but of course you can create your own guided visualization journey.

> *Begin by relaxing each part of the body in turn … first relax your fingers, now feel your hands relaxed … your wrists … and so on until you relax your whole body. Write down each part of the body in turn and literally ask yourself to relax each area one at a time. Then create a magical place to meet your angels. This can be anywhere you feel comfortable, and might include sitting on the seashore, waiting by a stream or chatting together in a meadow. Say to yourself, 'As I walk towards the wood [or beach or wherever your magical place is], I see my guardian angel ahead of me.'*
>
> *Give yourself the opportunity to ask your angel questions, and remember to leave a suitable gap for the answers on your recording. A 'journey' of around 20 minutes is probably sufficient at first. Record your own voice reading out your 'journey' and then play it back at*

a time when you can fully relax. If you prefer, you can ask a friend to read out the script for you, or you can have a browse around your local new age store or buy pre-recorded meditations online.

HEARING ANGELS

Angels usually communicate by sending us thoughts and feelings, but they can also sometimes communicate in words. Usually these words arrive as a sort of thought-transference, a mind-to-mind message (telepathy). Angels don't actually have voice boxes so don't talk in the traditional human way!

On occasion, angels communicate with music (said to be produced as a form of praising of the Lord). I once heard this amazing sound – in the bathroom at home (I wasn't drunk, I promise!). After my daughter became ill one night I asked the angels (rather rudely as it happened) to help her. My response was to hear the unbelievable sound of a celestial choir filling the air. Rather than be filled with awe at the startling sound, as you might expect, I was initially a little confused and looked for a more logical explanation … I found none!

I can easily see how angels gained a reputation for sitting on clouds playing harps all day … if the beautiful harmonies that I heard are anything to go by, then I can see why others may have come to this conclusion.

Some have been lucky enough to hear this music when they were children or when sitting with the dying or recently deceased. Some say that the angels are carrying their loved ones safely home to the 'other side' of life when they hear this sound, or that the angels are simply alerting us to their presence. Occasionally people hear the sound of the angels in particularly beautiful places, or perhaps for no apparent reason at all!

Here is another letter on the subject … with many questions.

Bright Blessings, Jacky

Many thanks for your beautiful website and offer of help to those in need. I will try to be brief as I am very ill at the moment with severe ME [Myalgic Encephalomyelitis, also known as Chronic Fatigue Syndrome].

I believe in angels and I've twice heard them singing in 'their language' while I've been lying in bed.

I try to pray to them daily, but can you please tell me how to find the name of my guardian angel? I keep asking but to no avail. Maybe it's because I am so ill that I'm blocking their messages. Hopefully you can help me. I feel so desperate all the time spending most of each day in bed. I sometimes feel they aren't there at all.

Please, please help me to connect. Also, which particular angel should I call on to help me heal? I have lots of angel books, cards, etc., but discovered you in a magazine article. I would dearly love to do the same sort of work as you. Who knows, perhaps one day?

Please reply to my email personally. I know you must be bombarded, and I truly wish you Joy and Love.

Blessed Be.

Carroll, Ireland

Hello, lovely lady

Thank you for your kind words about my website. I do indeed love what I do and I know I am lucky! But I do believe we create our own luck and we each create our own path (co-created with the highest source) … and I know that you can do this work too if you really want to.

I can't imagine how frustrating it is for you to suffer with ME. Take this very much as a signal from your guides, and take the rest that is being forced onto you ... but not in the way that you think!

I am hearing the angel name 'Avril' (I am not sure she minds what you call her!) and I feel drawn to ask you to look at the Out of Body Experience websites on the internet. It is actually possible to learn to lift your soul free from your body … soul travel or astral projection (something to learn while you are stuck in bed).

Meditation techniques can help you to develop your psychic ability, so that when you're too ill to walk out of bed you can fly out, using your new-found ability to soul-travel! (I did this a few years ago, I'm not kidding!) In bed you have the chance of developing your psychic ability. It's a lot of work and you may want to do this at your own pace, so take this 'opportunity' that has presented itself. What is that phrase? If you have lemons, make lemonade?

What a wonderful gift you had when hearing the angelic choir; this is a sure sign that the angels are working with you right now. For many people, including myself, hearing this beautiful music begins a lifelong quest for spiritual knowledge and transformation.

I don't believe that your ME will make it more difficult for you to communicate with your angels – actually I feel the reverse might be true, as you have the time to be still, to listen within yourself.

The Archangel who helps with healing is Raphael. Ask the Archangel Raphael to sit with you, alongside your own guardian angels. You don't need to pray to the angels (only God), so talk to your angels as you would a dear friend.

All the best to you.

Jacky x

LETTING US KNOW THEY ARE AROUND

Angels are happy to give us a little clue that they are around if we ask them to. They don't want to frighten humankind, so their signs are usually delicate or restrained … like this story. Carol had been asking her angels for a clue that they were with her, and she got her response in a fun way.

Dear Jacky

A few weeks ago I emailed you regarding an article of yours I had seen in a magazine. I left the copy of the magazine I was reading for a few minutes, and when I came back to it the page had turned to the article entitled, 'Someone to watch over you'.

Something else strange has just happened. My husband bought a juke box a couple of weeks ago. This afternoon he was loading CDs onto it, then played a couple of tracks. That was about three hours ago. Just now I was in the kitchen when I heard the juke box start up. My husband Roger was in the bathroom shaving, so I called and asked him if he had put a CD on, but he hadn't. There was no one else about. It started playing on its own, which is impossible because you have to select the tracks. It was playing a song recorded by Cher … the title? 'Believe'!

The really weird thing is that as I sat down to write this email it started playing again, this time another Cher CD. The title of this track is 'Does Anybody Really Fall in Love Anymore?' and there is a line in the song which goes ' … Looking for an angel …'

What's even more amazing is the juke box played both tracks when it had no 'credits' registered on it – which is impossible.

I hope you find this interesting.

Best wishes.

Carol W

Dear Carol

It is easy to put some of this down to coincidence, isn't it? But usually what happens is that people receive several small signs together, which when combined seem to suggest that there is more here than meets the eye!

Did your angel play the juke box for you? Who knows, but no doubt they will still bring you more signs to illustrate their point!

After my own dad passed he regularly played certain tracks that became 'his songs'. Sometimes if his song came on the radio the sound would become louder, noticeably quieter or even stop mid-track. Many times I woke in the morning to 'hear' his song playing in my head, and I wasn't the only one. Other

relatives had this same phenomenon happen to them too!
Jacky

P.S. As I typed this reply my font suddenly changed to capital letters – I have no idea why (another sign? Maybe they wanted to make the point).

More of these stories can be found in the afterlife section. Our loved ones also like to have fun with electrical items and mess around with electric lights, televisions, computers and even telephones, so be open to just about anything! If they can make it work they will.

FEELING ANGELS

Angels sometimes make themselves known to us by touching us physically in some way. This might come as the feel of a comforting hand taking your hand, or perhaps a hand on your shoulder.

Hi Jacky
Don't know if you could explain this one, but I hope you can. My partner is going through a rough patch at the moment, and nothing seems to be making him happy. His problems are the usual stuff like work, the house, himself (nonsense about his age) and so on.

I've been trying to meditate and have bought a set of angel cards and one of the cards that kept on popping out for him was the freedom card. The description was that he was the only person holding himself back (or something like that).

Anyway, one night I was downstairs (he was asleep in bed) and I was sitting with the candles lit and listening to my angel music CD when I decided to ask for some help for him. The next day he told me that he hadn't been able to get to sleep and that he'd felt something kiss him! He thought it was me and he turned in the direction of the kiss (no doubt to tell me to get lost!) and saw an apparition which was a bluish-white colour.

He said he couldn't work out whether it was male or female, but he could make out the outline of a face. Then he said it floated for a couple of minutes and then disappeared through the wall.

He didn't feel scared or anything. I told him it must have been his guardian angel. Was it? Hope you can shed some light.

Thanks.

Chyrel, Italy

Hi Chyrel

Sometimes it is difficult to decide if an experience is an angel or our own dear spiritual guides, but this is one of those occasions when it doesn't really matter. What a lovely and positive response to your request for your husband.

Just accept it for the wonderful experience that it was, and don't worry about explanations. The reason? A simple message of love and support – I'm glad your husband wasn't frightened by his experience.

Jacky

OFFERING COMFORT

I love to read stories where people have been reassured or comforted by their guardian angels. This lovely story comes from Michelle.

Dear Angel Lady

I have a strange story to tell you. At first I thought it was God, but maybe it was my spirit guides or maybe my mother or even an angel?

Often I will ask God to send me a message. Not that I need proof that he is real, but just something so that I can feel his love for me. One day as I was walking through the parking lot of the place where I worked, I decided to ask God to send me a message. I just wanted to feel his grand love again. It rejuvenates my spirit.

Grand is the best word I have to describe how he is, and how he feels. Anyway, getting back to my story: I proceeded to go in to work and start my shift. I was about halfway through and, to be honest, I had forgotten my earlier request. I was at the register and nobody was in my line (I think I had just finished counting the money in my till drawer) and when I turned around there was one of those balloons ... you know, the really colorful fancy ones.

At first it was right behind me, but when I turned around it was right in front of me. It just stayed there right at eye level. It didn't have enough helium in it to keep it up high with the rest of the balloons, and it had escaped from where all of the other balloons were being contained. The really strange thing is that this balloon had a message on it. It was heart shaped, and it said 'PS. I Love you.'

When I turned around and saw it, it kind of startled me because it was just as if it were a person standing there next to me, saying 'I love you'! It stayed by my register for a long time and it was like the balloon was watching me. It stayed at eye level just like another person was there quietly watching and letting me know how they felt.

It stayed by my register for a good couple of hours before someone did something with it. At the time

I didn't have any money or I would have brought it home with me.

I also feel that God and the angels talk to me through the radio. He's talked to me personally on several occasions and I get goose bumps just remembering how 'grand' he is. I guess I just ask my spirit guides and my mother in the same way, right? Will I be able to differentiate who's who?

Thank you for listening to my story. God bless all of us.

Love, Michelle, USA

Dear Michelle

They say 'God moves in mysterious ways,' right? What a fun experience you had.

Yes it is always OK to ask for your loved ones, angels and spiritual guides to communicate with you if you want them to, but do remember that you cannot demand it. If it is right for you, then you will receive a sign – but don't worry if nothing happens immediately!

Be open to anything rather than looking for a specific sign, which may not be possible at the moment. It might not always be easy to tell who is who at first, but you will certainly feel that loving energy around you like a spiritual hug.

Love, Jacky

Chapter 4

More Angel Questions

'Every visible thing in this world
is put in the charge of an Angel.'
St Augustine

SAVING LIVES

Many of my readers write and tell me that angels have helped them in times of trouble. They sense, feel, see or hear someone with them. Some people might call these feelings 'gut instinct' or intuition.

Are these real angel encounters? Not every experience is gentle and whispered. For those who doubt, there are encounters that come 'smack' right in your face!

Dear Angel Lady

I just got back from holiday in Egypt. The holiday didn't start off that well because we were only 15 minutes into the flight when two birds flew into the engines! The pilot had to turn around so that we could land the plane again.

We were told that the plane was badly damaged and so we had to get off and wait for another flight out. Thinking ourselves very lucky that we'd reached the ground safely, we didn't mind waiting the extra 12 hours so much!

On the last night of our holiday we went into town to meet up with two of the workers who were on the boat we had been on all week (it was a scuba-diving holiday). We had a drink with them and then went to look in a souvenir shop. My dad wasn't feeling too well but me and my sisters wanted to stay at the shops for a little longer and we reassured him that we would be fine going back to the hotel by ourselves. My dad wouldn't let us, he said it wasn't safe and so, a bit sad, we went back to the hotel. He just felt that he wanted us with him.

Half an hour later I'd just closed my eyes when I heard a deep rumble and the doors shook. My sisters shot up, wondering what had just happened, then four minutes later the same thing happened again. I thought it was maybe a small earthquake, but within five minutes we got a call from my mum back home saying there had been a bomb where we were staying! We reassured her we were OK, but couldn't help thinking ourselves very lucky to have yet again escaped what could have been the end of us.

The next day we found out the explosions had been where we were earlier that night. It makes you wonder, maybe someone is watching over us.

Vicky, England

Hi Vicky

It certainly looks as if someone was watching over you that night, doesn't it? And the whole holiday, come to think of it. What an awful shock – well, two shocks. I hope that no one was hurt in the explosion and I am glad you got home safely.

In any major accident or dangerous situation like this there are always people who seem to make a dramatic escape. As people say, 'It's simply NOT your time!'

Sadly when people are hurt or killed it's difficult to understand why this might happen ... we have to trust that in some cases it's just part of a bigger plan for human souls. It's sad to think that when others intervene and take another life (as in the case of the bombing) that it probably was NOT someone's 'time'.

I make a point of asking for angels to help look after these souls and to comfort those left behind. If you are aware of others who may have been hurt or killed during your holiday, then you can do the same.

Take care and best wishes,

Jacky

PROTECTING US

Do angels help to protect us? I'm sure they do … and Vicky certainly seems to think so. So does Bernadette.

Dear Jacky

I have just read one of your books and I really loved it. It's a book that I'll keep referring to over and over again. While I was reading about how angels have helped people in danger, I remembered something that happened to us when my daughter Claire was three years old (she's now 26).

My best friend was visiting and Claire was upstairs playing. We were downstairs chatting when we heard Claire fall down the stairs. For what seemed like minutes, but was actually only seconds, we were frozen to the spot. Fearing the worst, we both dashed into the hallway and there was Claire on her knees smacking the steps that she had just fallen down and saying 'Naughty, naughty!'

I now believe that the angels saved her from a nasty accident that day. THANK YOU, ANGELS.
Bernadette, Scotland

Strangely enough (and maybe this is a good warning here), I've had many similar stories sent to me of children falling down stairs. Witnesses have seen children 'float' to the bottom or slow down in mid-air – some have even witnessed spirits who appeared and then disappeared immediately after the child landed safely. Just to be on the safe side, though, do make sure that your stairs are properly secure … just in case.

COMMUNICATING WITH ANGELS

Many books offer suggestions for communicating with angels (including my own), but these are just that: suggestions. Ultimately we don't have to follow fancy rituals if we don't want to, and sometimes the simplest approaches are the best. There is no right or wrong way to do it, just work with love and you can't go far wrong.

Hi Jacky
My name is Gina and I talk to the angels before I go to sleep, but I never know if I am doing it right, and don't know which angel to ask for. Could you please help me out?

Also, could you tell me, is there anything I need to say before I start talking to them or asking for help? I look forward to hearing from you, thanks.
Gina, Ireland

Hi Gina
Just talk to your angels the way you would a special friend. Always say please and thank you – then just chat away however you wish! Your angels will hear you.

If you want to create a special ritual, then you could light a candle, burn scented incense or play angelic-type music. The choice is yours … but you don't have to!
Jacky

ANGELS WITH MANY ROLES

Not everything that we ask our angels for has to be a 'life or death' thing. People do credit their angels with all sorts of interesting activities!

Dear Jacky
Hello, my name is Jody and I came to your lecture in Craig-Y-Nos. I found it really interesting. I have been studying my angels for a while now and I feel that I am getting a lot of information from them.

I bought a book about the angels and it had an exercise on a 'wake-up call', so I decided to have a go. I asked my angels to wake me up in the morning at 6.30, and they did!
Jody, Wales

I have several readers who've tried this – give it a go (perhaps you could practise by asking the angels to wake you up five minutes before your normal alarm goes off). Do your angels help you with unusual tasks? I would be interested to hear your stories, so drop me a line.

YOUR GUARDIAN ANGEL'S NAME

Why do we need to know the name of our Guardian Angels? Well, the answer is that we don't, but as we are only human we want to know! Let's face it, it's likely to be easier to build a relationship with 'someone' when we know who they are, and the first step to doing this is to have a name to work with.

I have edited my reply to this next letter so that I do not repeat what I have already covered earlier in the chapter.

Dear Angel Lady
I know my angels are close by. I pray to my angel or to an Archangel most days. I would love to connect

with my angel more ... or even find out my angel's name. I am going to two angel workshops soon, but wondered if I could find out my angel's name sooner.

Thank you.

Rosa, Spain

Hello, Rosa

Probably the easiest thing to do is to sit in quiet contemplation (meditation) and just ask for communication to come to you as an inspirational thought. Try relaxing, then ask your angel for his or her name. Take the first name that comes to mind – but if you do not like this, then feel free to change it (as I tell people over and over again, your angel will not mind).

Sometimes angels' names sound like what we might expect an angel to sound like, (with the traditional 'ael' or 'iel' on the end – which means 'of the Lord'), but other times we may hear a 'normal' human name like Sally or Tim … or Rosa!

Angels do not really have names and often pick a name which they feel we may feel confident with, so go ahead and use what works for you.

Best wishes,

Jacky

ASKING ANGELS FOR THEIR HELP

You can ask angels to help with all sorts of things. I do receive a lot of letters from people who feel they have nowhere left to turn and believe that their angels are the only ones who can help them. This faith is often strong.

A UK morning TV show once did a survey which indicated that more people turn to their guardian angels when they are in trouble than to a friend, counsellor or doctor!

I believe that angels work best when they are helping us to help ourselves, rather than immediately taking away a problem for us. This way we can learn and grow from each thing that we live through. Our souls become stronger. Often a problem feels like it is 'running away from us', though, and we don't know where to start.

I don't normally offer intimate advice and usually try to make suggestions for people so that they might work out their own solutions. With this letter I felt drawn to offer a little more, as if the angels were leading me.

Hi,

My name is Ian and I would like to know who my guardian angel is. I have severe financial difficulties at this present moment in time, and desperately need some form of guidance as I just don't know which way to turn or what to do to make things right. So much uncertainty surrounds me at the moment, something I find very hard to cope with.

A lot of horoscopes are indicating a positive change ahead, something I do believe will happen, it's just that things seem so volatile at the moment and the vision I'm getting is blurred. I need it to be clear. I feel extremely stressed with worry, as I have a wife and family to support whom I love dearly.

I have a great sense of pride in everything I do, and feel as though some of this is being taken away because I work hard and no matter whatever I do still cannot seem to make ends meet. Please can my guardian angel help me?

Many thanks,

Ian, England

Hi Ian

I feel great empathy with your problem and I am so sorry that you have so much stress in your life. Financial worries are a common life theme and many people are working through money difficulties at this time. Many believe we choose our challenges before we are born. Certainly, learning to live with less might well lead one down a more spiritual path. 'Things' aren't everything.

The important thing is to be honest with what you have right now and make sure you remove debt from your life. The priority is to find a financial advisor who can help you work through your finances as you decide what you can afford ... and what you can't. Don't try and tackle this alone – make a list of all money that is being spent and the income that is coming into the house. The Archangel Gabriel can assist in clear communication while you do this, so ask for Gabriel's assistance.

The sum is always a simple one. We earn more or spend less. A little of both is usually the best balance. Immediately facing up to what you can no longer afford is a good place to start – especially with the current state of the world economy. It's time for us all to tighten our belts and start working with cash!

Are you enjoying your work at the moment? Is it time for you and your wife to sit down and talk about other ways of living? You know your angels can help you, but they are not going to take away this 'challenge'. They encourage you to look at your own ideas but they will be there to support you every step of the way! Make the first step and the rest will be easier.

You may well have placed this 'challenge' into your life at this time because it was time for you to make some changes in your life at this point in time. (All work and no play is not a good balance.)

Could you consider moving to a less expensive house or just somewhere which works better for your family at this time in your life? Maybe you are interested in looking at a different type of career or a way to make a stress-free second income? Perhaps investments are what you need? Ask Archangel Michael to assist you and help lead you to the right answers.

Talk everything through with your wife and do this as a couple. Work together because this is your greatest strength. Be calm and reasonable and work out changes for less hassle and more power in your lives together. If you are unhappy, then others in your family will be, too.

You have the ability to do anything you want in your life. I believe in you. Know that your angels are right behind you. Maybe a few days away together will give you time to decide where you go next in your life. Be excited about these changes.

Get out a big pad of paper and pens – even the children can have some say (you would be amazed at their ideas, so don't discount anything, just write down everything as you brainstorm together). Later go through the list and give things a number priority between 1 and 10. Look at everything which gets a 7 or above as a 'priority'.

I do feel the Archangel Michael is already working with you at this time, as he regularly works with money issues. Feel free to call upon his help whenever you feel the need. I also hear the angel name 'Timmoni' (a new one on me, so probably your Guardian Angel!).

Good luck to you and your lovely family.

Jacky

OFFERING ADVICE

I believe that sometimes we have to go through a little pain in our lives to grow spiritually. I did say 'a little'. There is no reason why we should spend our lives suffering, as some people believe! During these more difficult times in our lives we become stronger people as we deal with problems and work through them.

Angels are not allowed to interfere with our life lessons. We are the ones who decide what we want to learn before we are born. Maybe that choice was courage or patience. You might not think you know what your life experiences are but I bet you do! Have a look at the words below and see if any of them jump out at you.

- Humility
- Patience
- Charity
- Tolerance
- Confidence

- Empowerment
- Self-esteem
- Inner Peace
- Fidelity
- Conscientiousness
- Kindness

Of course, this is just a very short list; there are many more things that we can choose to work on in each lifetime. Most of us come with one or two main goals and our life experiences help us achieve our goals. I also believe that, sometimes, a chosen experience might not go quite as we planned – it certainly helps to have a little divine intervention! Angels can lessen the burden a little – when we have taken on more than we can 'chew' or more than is necessary to grow from the experience.

Mother Teresa once said that God never gives us more than we can handle … but she also said that she wished that God didn't trust her so much! Good point. What are your own life lessons? Write down your insights for future reference.

LIVING YOUR BEST LIFE

Of course, not everything that happens in our lives is planned in advance, so don't start writing me letters to say you are having a bad time. No, of course it's not always your fault, but we do co-create our lives, so it's important that you handle each situation correctly!

Of course we also have roles to play in 'teaching' others and helping them achieve their goals and life lessons, but it's not what happens to you that is as important as what you do with the experience!

You have choices about how you feel and deal with life. Here is a life experience which I want to show you could turn out either of two ways, depending on Joyce's personal feelings and actions.

The Experience

Joyce was miserable. She worked long hours and had much debt in her life. She constantly felt ill. She had lived in the same house on her own for ten years and it needed much work. One Friday afternoon she went into work and was made redundant. Could anything be worse? What happens now?

Option 1. Joyce was devastated at losing her job and she hid herself away in the home she hated, spending more and more time in bed. Feeling more and more depressed, Joyce started to ignore her bills and rarely left the house. The garden became overgrown, she didn't answer the door when friends called, and eventually she lost her house. Joyce never recovered from the experience and always felt that the world was against her.

Option 2. Although Joyce was shocked at first, she realized that losing her job was the opportunity she had been waiting for. No longer tied to a location and a property she hated, she could now do anything she wanted. Nothing was going to hold her back.

Joyce spent the next couple of weeks painting her property and clearing out old belongings that no longer had a purpose in her life. Friends flocked to help Joyce after she asked for their help and the whole experience was full of joy and fun.

As she cleared the clutter in her life it reflected back in her body. She felt free and the objects she chose to keep were only those that she loved and were useful to her.

Joyce sold her old property and bought a smaller, modern apartment. Now that she had discarded old possessions that were cluttering up her life she didn't have to pay out for a big property to store her stuff. She chose her new home closer to the family she loved.

With the extra money she had freed up she took an art class and eventually set up her own crafts business.

OK, I had fun with the ending there, but you get my point. She could just have easily taken a job on a cruise ship and sailed around the world, or trained as a vicar. The same situation handled two different ways. Option 1 saw Joyce as a victim. Option 2 saw Joyce taking control of her life (with a little help from her friends). You don't have to lose your job to make these changes in your life.

House too expensive? Hate your job? What do you WANT to do? Ask your angels to help you write your own list of options … and don't forget to create your own happy ending.

Don't be a victim – start co-creating your life today!

Jill wrote and told me about a potentially terrifying experience but her angels were waiting on guard!

Dear Jacky

Many years ago when I was 24 and had just moved to a college town to work at the local radio station, I had no food, so I ran to the grocery store after work to get some shopping. As I walked in I noticed a man with obvious learning disabilities standing outside, so I smiled at him. I didn't know it then, but he followed me into the store.

He came up behind me and started putting his hands all over me. My first reaction was to became angry, and then a bit afraid. I tried to hurry away, but he chased me, grabbed me and threw me against a shelf of food! He said, 'Don't you know a rape when you see one?'

That's when my mind rolled out of my head and I really didn't participate in the struggle. It was almost as if this was happening to someone else. Rather surprisingly, I was aware of people in the aisle near me, but they did nothing! Later, they told police they thought he was my husband!

Yet, in my head, I was told to scream for help, and apparently they could hear me in the store next door. Finally, the store butcher rushed up and saved me.

It was very scary, yet I knew the entire time I was safe. I also felt like the whole experience was totally set up, because I felt his strong presence when I saw him outside the store and actually made eye contact and smiled. It was surreal ... like the angel told me I was safe and to scream.

Jill, USA

LIFE MISSION AND BINGO ANGELS?

Many people want to know if the angels can help them with their life mission or life's purpose, like Janet. Janet also shares some of her own angel experiences in her letter; I've left these in for you to enjoy.

Hi Jacky

I have a story for you. Leading up to the time before I was actually contacted by the angels, I really didn't have much of an idea I was being followed. Many events have happened to me. Now I know I was being followed by the angels.

One night I was at bingo; earlier I had been to the library and picked up a book about angels. I can't remember the title. Anyway, I took the book to bingo with me. The book had numbers in it and it explained how angels sometimes want to give us messages by using numbers.

So I was in bingo reading the book when I came to the numbers 443 343 222. My bingo ticket had 443 on the side of it. I was playing the last three-page main book, when suddenly I felt a long beautiful stroke on my right arm. No words were spoken to me at the time. But I won on that ticket, on the numbers 443!

On another night my angel, which had a male voice, spoke to me while I was playing bingo. I really did jump when I heard his voice, it was so beautiful, Jacky. He told me to watch the board, while the numbers 222 came up.

The other thing I would like to add is that the book, after I took it back to the library, was missing the next time I went to take it out. I must add that clearly at the time my angels really wanted to make me aware of them.

Another time my angel put a feather behind my daughter's seat where she sits in bingo. I told my daughter she was going to win that night and she just smiled at me. She didn't believe me but my angel and I shared a secret. I knew she was going to do well that night.

She went on to win three times that night, Jacky, and I have come to know the angels so well.

Jacky, there is something I would like to ask you. I am to be given 'my mission' in the next two years … my life mission. I have no idea what I am supposed to do. I do know that I've been given a key to help people. Can you help me, Jacky, please? How do I know why I am here, why I was born … what is the purpose of my life?
Janet, England

Hi Janet
Your bingo angels sound fun! I'm sure many readers would like to borrow them for the night.

You know, your life mission is really very easy. What do you love doing? Working with God and the angels is more simple than you might believe.

God sends us to do what we are good at, and to work with our personal skills. Do you like healing? Talking? Decorating? Singing? Do what brings you most joy – use this in your service to God and the angels, and you won't go far wrong. Anything and everything are part of God's work. Everything is done with love and positive intent, following people's free will.

Use your gut instinct to make sure that you are being true to yourself and others, and off you go! Let me know how you get on.

Best wishes,
Jacky

PUTTING PEOPLE TOGETHER

Angels usually need permission to help us. When we let them know it's OK to help out they can assist us in many different ways. I love when they plan little 'coincidences' and put the right people together to create benefits for all parties concerned.

Often things turn out 'for the best', if only we can enjoy the ride and wait and see what happens next. We don't always get exactly what we want but the outcome the angels create can be far more beneficial than anything we could plan for ourselves.

In life we try to take control of every little thing which happens in our lives, but if you just wait … and trust, all the pieces will fall into place! Ask for that angelic intervention and then carry on as if you have no doubt that it will happen. The angels … and the universal energy … will bring the things you need to you.

When I was on holiday earlier in the year I stopped to have my hair cut one day. The hairstylist mentioned what a 'coincidence' it was that I had arrived, as several of the staff had been talking about various paranormal experiences that day.

We had quite a chat and she told me about her teenage son. Like many boys of his age, he had left school with no clear idea of where to go next. His parents, like most of us, had tried to rush their son out of bed each day and push him to start searching for a job. The young man was determined to stay put, though, and explained that he was going to take a few weeks off and that the perfect job would come to him.

His parents were not amused and his mother said that she quite clearly told her son, 'No one is going to come and knock on the door and offer you a job!' But her son was convinced otherwise, and for the next few weeks just relaxed around the house.

His parents were getting more and more worried but eventually their son felt ready for his new job. The very next day an old family friend came and knocked on the door … you guessed it … he offered their son a job! Coincidence? Ummmm … if you like!

Dear Jacky

To keep it short here ... my parents and another couple went to a small town to see a play. They had reservations at the only hotel in town, but when they got there the rooms were all filled, and there were no other hotels. The husband of the other couple got extremely angry, but my calm mother appealed to her angels and said '... I know there is a perfect place for us to stay.' That's when the hotel clerk said there was an elderly woman in town who rented rooms. She took them in, and

Mom said it was the loveliest house with gorgeous antiques and the woman was wonderfully kind and accommodating.

While they all sat and chatted that evening, the woman mentioned that her husband was a severe alcoholic. The husband of the other couple had recovered in the AA (Alcoholics Anonymous) program and he stayed up late helping this dear woman! Mom knows an angel brought them to the perfect place to stay.

Jill, USA

I like that phrase, 'the perfect place'. Ask your own angels for the perfect outcome to your own problems after stating what you need! Then let them work their magic … and of course write and tell me all about it so that I can share your magical experiences with the whole world! ☺

FEATHERS

I love it when angels leave feathers to let us know that they are close. Lots of you collect these beautiful white feathers which the angels leave as 'calling cards' and indications that they are around us and helping.

I'm not sure that the feathers in this story are the typical experience, though!

Dear Jacky

Last year my granddad was in hospital. I hate going to hospitals because I used to be in and out visiting Granddad all the time and I used to get upset seeing him in a bad way. This one time, I went with Mum, and outside the hospital there were lots of beautiful, small, white feathers and I instantly recognized the sign.

'Look, Mum, it's going to be OK, those feathers are a sign of an angel.'

Mum didn't seem too convinced, but was happy that I'd relaxed. Granddad told us that he could come out soon, as he was on the mend, so we were all really glad. On the way out back to the car, Mum started laughing.

'Look, Jess, there's your angel.'

In the middle of the road was a poor, mangled seagull and, sure enough, feathers were blowing all down the path. So this time my angels played a joke on me, but it still worked because I went into the hospital happier and more positive!

Jess

The story here has a positive ending just the same, but whether angels were at work here is hard to tell! Why wouldn't they make use of feathers that were nearby? It would certainly be more convenient! I too get a lot of feathers in my garden … but then I do have cats (I no longer feed the birds – I don't want to be responsible for this cat-buffet!).

What makes a feather an angel feather? My opinion is that the feather appears in an unusual place as a result of a request for a sign. Sometimes those feathers are white but people do tell me stories of unusual sightings of feathers in all sorts of colours! If it feels like an angel feather to you, then it probably is.

As far as I am aware, 'angel feathers' are simply normal feathers which have been utilized by an angel to pass on their message, rather than something the angels have actually shed from their own 'bodies', because, of course, real angels are made of light-energy … not bird-wings!

Dear Jacky

I have never experienced the feeling of angels until the birth of my triplets. I met a woman who was viewing my home. She told me that angels are all around me. She even gave me their names. I did not take her very seriously, until the feathers starting dropping from everywhere. Not just in my home but everywhere I went.

Our business has been down for a few weeks now, and I haven't thought about God or angels or anything! This evening I was at the cashier and feathers were surrounding my feet. There was this incredible sense of peace, and then I knew everything would be OK.

I placed the feathers on the bar and a server threw them in the trash, I took them out and explained to her a few things. The funny part of this story is that at the end of her shift one of the guests touched her shoulder and told her there was something on the back of her shirt … another feather!
Patrice, USA

Priceless!

Dear Jacky
My sister-in-law was at a spiritual church and there were two mediums and a chairperson, and in the background she saw black angels' wings. Can you tell me what this means?
Carol, England

Hi Carol
Sometimes people do see black feathers rather than the traditional white after asking for an angel sign, but this doesn't seem to have any adverse affect at all.

I've read several hundred 'feather stories' and have drawn some conclusions of my own. When people receive white feathers they mean, 'I'm with you … I'm here for you.' With black feathers it seems to acknowledge you are going through a difficult time already. So they are saying, 'We know you are in distress right now and we are here for you, already at your side.'

Just take it as a sign that angels have shown themselves. Usually people start a search to discover what this means to them ... and it begins a spiritual journey or psychic search for the truth as it occurs in their own lives. If you have a strong feeling that a feather has a different meaning for you, then you may be right. This is not an exact science.

Jacky

Others find feathers when they are not expected.

Hiya Jacky

When I walked into my office earlier this morning, I spotted a white feather in the corridor ... just before the entrance into our office.

I have always secretly wished that a sign would come through or appear, and have always believed that we have a guardian angel looking out for us. Do you think this has a logical explanation to it?

I half believe, but a part of me feels that there is an explanation to everything mystical. I would love to hear your thoughts on this.

Many thanks.

Joanne, England

Hi Joanne

Thank you for writing to me. Of course there is often an alternative explanation. Not everything unusual that happens has a mystical explanation. Feathers blow through the window and stick to people's clothes and shoes. It is always difficult to be objective about individual cases, but I believe that many of these experiences are being set up for us to start investigating a spiritual path.

As you can see, immediately we say, 'What was that?' and want to find out more! The fact that you noticed it probably says more about this case – you were drawn to the feather, it was brought to your attention. Of course you are right that not everything has a paranormal explanation, and we should always try and rule out any rational explanations to satisfy ourselves first of all.

Was your experience an angel? Did it create an interest in you for all things angelic? Quite possibly ... in which case it did the job anyway!

Good luck and best wishes,

Jacky x

I hope these chapters have whet your appetite. Now it's time for some of your fascinating real-life angel experiences!

Chapter 5

Angel Stories

'It is not known precisely where angels dwell – whether in the air, the void, or the planets. It has not been God's pleasure that we should be informed of their abode.'
Voltaire

Angel stories … true-life accounts of angel intervention, life-saving and life-changing visits from our guardians – I love them, and so do my readers. I have picked out a special selection.

WATCH THE BIRDIE

'During a night out with my family I was driving everyone home at around 2 a.m.; my family lives about 15 minutes out of the city. Since I had driven down the same road many times, my focus wasn't completely on the road but on everyone talking and laughing. Then suddenly, out of nowhere, a bird of some sort flew right out in front of the vehicle. It startled me so much that I gripped the steering wheel more tightly, reduced my speed and completely focused my attention on the road just in case anything else flew out of nowhere!

'A few moments later I noticed the back of an animal walk off the road and into the ditch. At first I thought that it was just a coyote, but as we neared the area of the road where we had seen the animal, two big deer casually walked across the road! It nearly frightened me to death. I was going about 80 km/h and only just had enough time and distance to hit the brakes … narrowly avoiding a big accident!

'I was shocked but realized afterwards how important that bird had been. If the bird hadn't startled me so much, I would probably have hit the deer. I daren't even begin to think of the outcome.

'I truly believe (and so do the others in the vehicle) that our guardian angels sent me a "warning" to be cautious and pay attention to the road! An impact of hitting two full-grown deer at 100 km/h – the normal speed for the road (even in an SUV) would have been disastrous!' – *Laura, Canada*

I've come across these 'warning' stories before. I believe that those on the other side of life have the ability to look ahead slightly and see what is 'likely' to happen, or 'most likely' to happen based on the current set of circumstances.

Because we always have the ability to modify our behaviour, we have the power to change the future in so many ways. Angels' help is imperative. Here is a little angel help in the workplace.

ANGEL AT LARGE

'For a while I found myself working with a very difficult person. She treated my young colleague and me with such contempt. Even though I was a lot older than her she never gave me any respect.

'Each day going to work was a trial. I knew we were going to feel her wrath and it made my life, at my normally happy job, become impossible when she was around.

'One morning I woke up and saw a huge man in my bedroom. I turned away and thought it was a trick of the light but when I looked again he was still there. He was about 7 feet tall and was dressed as if in biblical times. He was wearing a blue woollen jumper and a long white cotton skirt, he had a turban on his head and a short black beard. He stayed for about two or three minutes, then simply disappeared. I felt a sense of peace around him and I certainly didn't feel afraid. I told a friend of mine and she said it was probably my guardian angel who was acknowledging I needed his help.

'Each morning after that, I sent my angel into the office before me to soften this colleague's wrath. It really did work because it turned out that my young colleague and I were the only people in the office whom she became really friendly with. She changed her attitude and even apologized to us.

'Now whenever I'm afraid of something I remember my large masculine angel friend and send him on ahead. He has never failed me.' – *Patricia, Ireland*

Don't forget to ask your own angel for help with challenging situations in your own life. It's always useful to have a friend along to help.

GUARDIAN CAT ANGELS?

'A couple of years ago I was walking home in the early hours of the morning from a night out. The road was pretty quiet and I got a bit nervous even though I've walked home many times and never felt scared before.

'I decided to ask the angels to keep me safe and immediately after I did this I started to see one or two cats along my route … which isn't unusual, but then the strangest thing happened, I began to see groups of cats on the other side of the road too, lots of them. They were just watching me everywhere I went. They were not meowing or making a sound, just watching as I walked past them. Bizarrely I spotted more and more cats all the way home and it really made me feel that someone was keeping an eye on things. I said "Thank you" as I walked past them – it just seemed so surreal.

'When I reached the bottom of my street I didn't see any more cats, but I've always wondered to this day if angels can appear as animals. I've always loved animals and cats are my favourite.' – *Tanya, Wales*

This is an unusual story but perhaps the cats were angels in disguise. It certainly did the trick anyway and Tanya made it safely home.

Can angels help with money, do you think? Suzi thinks so, and wrote to tell me all about it.

MONEY, MONEY, MONEY

'I've believed in angels for many years, Jacky, but it seems the longer I believe the more they help me. I have many stories to tell you, but the one I am about to share has been going on for years!

'A few years ago it was Christmas Eve. Money was tight and it was a struggle to afford even essential items that you would buy every week in the supermarket, let alone all those special things you buy at Christmas.

'I went to the cashpoint at my local supermarket to withdraw the last £20 I had and waited my turn. As I approached the till I saw that the woman before me had forgotten to take her cash. I didn't hang around, Jacky,

I took it, folded it up and stuffed it in my jeans pocket. Other people, I'm sure, would have thought no more of it but for some reason I felt compelled to find the rightful owner and so I asked my angel to ask *her* angel to bring her to me. I decided that if she hadn't found me by the time I had finished my shopping, then I would think of it as a gift and keep it but spend it wisely.

'Moments later, a hand tapped me on the shoulder! I turned and a young woman said, "Excuse me, but did I leave my money in the cashpoint?" I asked her, "What till was it?" and "How much?" and she proved herself to me and so I returned the money.

'I have no right to sit in judgement of anyone, so I'll just say that she looked as if she needed it more than me. I admit I felt a bit sick about it all and wondered if my intentions weren't as honourable as I'd proclaimed!

'Off I went to the supermarket and did my shopping. Closing time was very near. When I got to the checkouts I realized that I'd never drawn any money from the cashpoint so I paid with my card. My shopping was only about £15 but to this day that transaction has never shown on my bank statement, Jacky, and that was several years ago.

'There's more ...

'About three years ago I was walking through the local shopping centre when there, lying on the floor as clear as day, was a wad of bank notes! I picked it up and walked off with it while I decided what to do with it. I asked once again for the rightful owner to be brought to me and, lo and behold, somehow a whole hour later he appeared. In the nearby market I heard him say, "Yeah I had it tucked in my passport, I took my hanky from my pocket in the Priory Centre and I reckon it must have dropped out there."

'I took him to one side and asked him if he'd lost some money and he said he had (who wouldn't?). As before, I asked him more details ... It was his, so I returned it and he gave me £20 for my honesty.

'After this I said to my angel could she please show me the lesson that she was trying to teach me in another way, as I was finding it harder and harder to give the money back! The next week I received a £500 tax rebate!

'Hmmmmmm' – *Suzi, England*

Angels don't always like to help with money, but they can. Mainly they prefer to help us to find ways of solving the problem – discovering long-term solutions. Although sometimes readers share stories of emergency cash (and food) appearing from mysterious means (especially when children are in need), so there are no hard-and-fast rules – just general ones!

ANGEL CROSSING GUARD

'One day I was venturing out on the normal mundane school run to collect my two wonderful children. On this particular day I felt very edgy for no particular reason but I proceeded to collect the children as normal.

'Suddenly I was aware of a van driving very fast down the road and I remember thinking "What a ridiculous speed" – then, to my horror and panic, I noticed my youngest child was standing in the road. Quick as a flash I saw an angel's wing shoot out and pull him back, preventing his certain death!

'Now you might think this is unbelievable, but I will now introduce some logic. This van was going at least 60 miles per hour – think about the stopping distance.

'Bizarrely, the vehicle came to an immediate stop … that was proof to me, but amazingly there were skid marks and the smell of burning rubber – again to prove how fast the car had actually been travelling.

'We all have a great fondness for angels and have a strong belief that they watch over us. I know that my son's life was saved by an angel that day.' – *Elizabeth, England*

This dramatic rescue must have left poor Elizabeth in shock … thank goodness her little one was OK.

DIPLOMATIC ASSISTANCE

'I feel very lucky to have experienced many signs and reassurances from my angels. I often see white feathers which float down so gently and always when I need them most. I feel that I am open to the many ways that they choose to communicate with me, and have used these experiences to convert many sceptical friends and family.

'My mum, who is also very spiritual, bought my sister and me a perpetual calendar which contained a different thought about angels for each day. During this time I was a student nurse and this involved placements on many different hospital wards.

'During a particular placement I was assigned a mentor who would be responsible for me while on the ward. The ward was extremely busy and it was a very daunting experience as a novice! From the offset I felt totally unsupported by my mentor. I kept telling myself that she was a very busy nurse and that things would improve, but I constantly felt as if I was just getting in her way and that I was a just a nuisance to her.

'I feel that I am quite a strong person and I'm able to think positively about most situations, but as the weeks progressed and things didn't improve, I began to really doubt my abilities as a nurse and dreaded going into work.

'During one particular shift my mentor had barely spoken to me and even during break would never try to make conversation. I left that night feeling so down, and cried most of the way home. When I arrived home I was certain I was not going back to the ward and was feeling so inadequate. However a phone call from my mum helped me to see things more clearly and I did go to work the following morning.

I can't begin to tell you how different this shift was. From walking onto the ward I could feel that something had changed, like a light had come on. My mentor greeted me so nicely that I was taken aback, and she explained that she had arranged for me to follow a patient to theatre and stay for the operation. I left that day feeling so different to the night before, like I was at last starting to find my role within the team.

'When I arrived home, the first thing I did was call my mum. During the conversation she asked what my calendar had said that morning. I realized I had run out of the house without turning it over, something I do religiously each morning. The verses are so uplifting, but I had never had one so specific. It had both my mum and me in tears. I felt that I was meant to read it then, as it would not have meant half as much to me if I'd read it before work: "A surgeon's hand, a friend's note, and a mentor's pat on the back are all angels in the guise of the ordinary – carrying us like a thousand lifting wings."

'I could not ask for a clearer sign that I have an angel providing me with constant protection and love. It's a lovely feeling to have when you feel low at points in your life.' – *Kathryn, Ireland*

These wonderful 'coincidences' are a regular communication tool from the angels. Watch out for synchronicity (meaningful coincidences) in your own life … and note them down for future reference.

CAUTION!

'One Monday afternoon I was driving my daughter and her friend back from their usual swimming class. While I was driving I saw myself talking on the phone to my husband, saying, "You must come now, I know Amy is in her pyjamas but just bring her with you, you have to come now." In my mind's eye I was standing outside my friend's driveway, with the car in the road. My daughter's friend lives on a very busy road and vision is not very good when pulling out of the driveway. I realized right away that this was a warning.

'So I dropped off the friend, and with great CAUTION I slowly drove down the driveway towards the road. Well, I'm so glad. I would normally drive right onto the pavement at the end of the drive, but because of my caution I narrowly missed a cyclist who was cycling by with another car overtaking at the same time!

Well, my heart missed a beat when I realized I could so easily have knocked down the poor boy on the bike. I'm so glad I listened to the warning. If I had driven onto the pavement, the cyclist would have hit the side of my car, followed by the car that was overtaking him.

'How lucky we all were. I don't know who showed me that vision ... my angel, my guides, any one of my deceased relatives? But I am thankful they did.

'I've never had a vision like that before and I said a special prayer of thanks that day. I promise to listen more, whenever they want to tell me something.' – *Jeni, England*

Where do these visions come from? It really makes you think, doesn't it? Are these messages from our guardian angels, or some sort of premonition? Remember, if we change our actions it is sometimes possible to change the 'future'. Just recall my phrase 'you are the co-creator of your world' (I'll keep reminding you). It certainly doesn't do any harm to drive safely in any regard.

MOTORBIKE GUARDIAN

'In 2003 my teenage son Mikey was living with his dad. His father bought him a motorbike, which I hated. I told him I didn't want to see or hear about it and that was the way that I coped.

'On the morning of Wednesday 11th June, I woke up after having the weirdest dream. The dream was so vivid I told my husband about it. He just laughingly said, "You and your dreams!"

'All throughout the day at work the dream was still as vivid and I told a couple of my friends about it. I dreamt that a Chinese woman was giving birth to a baby, but the baby was wearing a motorbike helmet. The helmet was yellow with splashes of other colours over it.

'After work that evening Mikey popped round for something to eat. When he was leaving I went to the door with him and realized he'd ridden over on his motorbike. I was upset and told him to take it right back to his dad's.

'As I walked into the living room, I could see Mikey through the window. He was putting on a yellow helmet with splashes of colour over it. I screamed to my husband, "Oh, my God, it's the helmet in my dream, he's going to kill himself on that bike." (I remembered being told years before that if you dream of a birth it means death and vice versa.)

'Before I had a chance to tell Mikey to get off the bike, he'd gone. I went to follow him, and when I caught him up I told him to put the bike away and not to ride it. He kept asking why so I told him about the dream even though it sounded so silly. Mikey just laughed but he could see how upset I was, so he promised to stop riding it. I was so relieved.

'The following day he asked if he could ride his bike again and I told him no, then the day after that he asked me again, and again I said no. I was too worried.

'Mikey came shopping with me after work to get some food for a barbecue; we were going to stay at our caravan. Mikey decided at the last minute he didn't want to come with us, so I agreed with his dad that Mikey could stay overnight with him.

'I was worried about leaving Mikey and the dream was still very much on my mind but I couldn't get him to change his mind. The last words I said to him before I left were, "Mikey, promise me you won't ride that motorbike."

'"I promise," he replied. So we left for the caravan. There was nothing more that I could do.

'In the early hours of the morning I was woken by a phone call from my daughter. Mikey had been in a terrible motorbike accident. He had multiple injuries and the news was bad.

'"Mum, the doctors don't think he'll survive ..." I was in complete and utter shock as I tried to listen to the details. The accident had happened right by a Chinese restaurant and I immediately recalled the Chinese symbolism in my dream.

'Mikey went through 16 hours of surgery that night. Somehow he managed to survive his initial operation. Many more were to come. Mikey had nearly decapitated himself, sustaining serious damage to his throat. Surgeons performed an operation which had never been done before. In every other case, this type of accident had resulted in death.

'Then disaster struck. After 36 hours, Mikey died ... but after ten minutes they revived him again. His brain was actually starved of the oxygen it needed for over 40 minutes and the doctors were very concerned at the outcome. Yet a nurse seemed convinced, "There's someone up there looking after your son," she said. I really hoped so.

'I was still in shock. We had already been through so much but we had no idea whether Mikey would live or die or, even if he did live, what quality of life he might have.

'I went outside the hospital and found a place to gather my thoughts, but as I sat down I noticed a beautiful white feather spiral down and land by my feet. My niece told me the feather was a gift from the angels, but I had never heard of this before. I carefully picked the feather up and kept it. A few months later I found another white feather on Mikey's bed. This one was identical to the one I'd found outside. This was more than coincidence, I was sure of it.

'Mikey survived. The doctors called him a miracle but I was sure that he'd had a little help from the angels. Then two years after the accident my son was talking to his friends about what had happened, and one of them asked him what it was like to die. I was shocked to hear his friend ask him such a question, but even more shocked when I heard Mikey's reply: "It was so peaceful. I found myself going up some stairs. It was really bright … really lovely. I wanted to carry on going but there was a man at the side telling me I had to go back. I told him I didn't want to, but he said that I had to. The next thing that happened was like I heard and felt a big BANG. I felt myself falling and everything was just loud and noisy again," Mikey recalled.

'I was stunned and later asked him if he knew who the man was who had told him to "go back". Mikey didn't know but he could describe him very clearly. Mikey told me the man was thin with black hair. My father was thin with black hair, and had died from cancer when Mikey was 11 weeks old. I wonder if the angels had enlisted Dad's help to send my son back to me. What a miracle!

'Oh, and by the way … I still have those angel feathers!'
– *Donna, Wales*

Many people dream of births and death. Sometimes dreaming of a birth can mean a 'new beginning' and dreaming of a death can indicate the end of an old situation, so don't think that if this happens to you that it means that someone is going to die (or be born). There are many variations.

And remember, sometimes a dream is just a dream!

HEALING ANGEL

'I have recently been diagnosed with cancer in the spine and I've had a bad time with treatments. When I was at my lowest ebb an angel came to me and clearly said, "You will be all right." This was the Archangel Michael. He appeared one night in the doorway of my bedroom.

'My angel encounter was the turning point for me and I am indeed blessed to have him near me. During my illness I say all the time "Fill my body with light and love" and it works.

'My treatment has finished and I now have checks only every two months, and I am fine. The angels are truly wonderful and I know are there for me when I call.' – *Barbara, England*

Angels often appear during illness and accidents. I love the comfort they bring to those in need.

A BEAR ANGEL?

'I hope you don't mind reading long stories. Not that my experience is a long one, but I always seem to take forever to explain things.

'My name is Frederick and I'm 19 years old. I never really believed in angels. Sure, I am interested in paranormal stuff, but angels never really seemed that realistic to me. I was more one to believe in aliens or fate or destiny; that everyone has a purpose in life and that somehow some force is trying to show us.

'The I met Emily and we became very close friends – and we still are. At one point I made something for her on the computer. I took one of her pictures and made some art by making her look like an angel. Anyway, I thought that there was something missing so I finished it off by typing, "Like an angel on my shoulder".

'One night I had this dream. I was in a dark, empty space and before me in a clear light stood a "goth" girl. I could only see the whites of her eyes. She was blind, and floating next to her was what looked like a "ghost bear".

'She talked in a language I didn't recognize – if I had to guess I would say Polish – but somehow I did understand what she said. She told me her name was "Tear" and that she was blind, but that she could see through the eyes of Christopher (the bear). He protects her as she protects me. I had a feeling of enlightenment by her presence. When I woke up I wondered what the crazy dream was about and why I had been able to dream so clearly.

'I started thinking that Tear could be my guardian angel, although I thought it was ridiculous since I didn't believe in that stuff. I tried drawing her and I still have that sketch on my computer. I thought about it more and more, but I kept denying it.

'Then I bought a book and it taught me to think differently. It said that you have to imagine two people, one good and one evil, being next to you all the time. This would help, because you would be able to see what thoughts were negative and which were positive. I know this probably sounds a bit stupid, but my thoughts were a mess and it made me able to clean them up a bit. I decided to use Tear as my good person and within a couple of weeks I was better.

'I didn't believe she was an angel until I noticed another book. It was a copy of your book *An Angel Saved My Life*. Normally the book wouldn't have caught my eye, but they translated the title into Dutch differently: *Een engel op mijn schouder*. Translated into English that's "An angel on my shoulder". Because of the title (reminding me of the "art-piece" I'd made) I read the back of the book. Even though angels didn't really appeal to me, somehow I got the feeling that I had to read it, so I bought it and took it home.

'Now, after reading the book I think somehow fate has led me this way. I think the book and translation of the title were fate's way of showing me that Tear really is my guardian angel. Maybe the language she spoke was one of a higher spiritual kind or something like that.' – *Frederick, Belgium*

Dreams are often the catalyst for change, and angels can and do make appearances in many different ways – although this is the first time I have been told about a 'bear angel', I'm sure it won't be the last!

HEAVEN'S GARDENS

'My mother died at the end of June last year, age 61, six months after being diagnosed with lung cancer. The last month of her life she spent in a hospice. I stayed with her almost 24/7 during that time, and it was the most precious time we shared together. My mum and I had a strong connection, especially as my father had died when I was eight.

My mother didn't believe that much in an afterlife. I always asked her to give me a sign if there was something like a Heaven, or an afterlife. And she did.

'My mother wasn't fully conscious during the last weeks of her life, but in the moments that she was, she sometimes said beautiful things that have strengthened me in my belief in the afterlife and helped me cope with my grief.

'She said, "There are beautiful gardens in Heaven ... I've been there ... blue flowers, and red ones, and white ones ... Oh, it's so pretty there."

'That was about two weeks before she died. I remember asking her if she would go there soon. She answered with, "No, silly. Not yet."

'A couple of days before she died, I asked her if she had visited the gardens again. "Yes, but it was a different garden now. There were all these strangers, greeting me."

'A friend of my mother had had her father in the same hospice several months before my mother was there. He'd been in the same room as my mother. When I told her about what my mother had said, she simply said: "My father has seen the gardens, too."

'After my mother's death I felt her presence a lot. She also sent me a vision of her, with a bright smile on her face, surrounded by flowers and nature. I think she wanted to show me that she is where she needs to be now.' – *Femke, The Netherlands*

Visions of the heavenly gardens do appear in many case histories on my files. They are commonly seen during near-death experiences and when we are close to death (but at other times, too, like when we are unconscious).

It's not unusual for people to see colours that don't exist on the earthly plane, too (or perhaps they do exist but our physical eyes are unable to interpret these colours even though our spirits can?). Flowers, trees and bodies of water in heaven appear alive and with consciousness. The gardens are always described as beautiful or even breathtaking!

Now let's explore some of your questions about the afterlife.

Chapter 6

Your Questions about the Afterlife

'We can never really know. I simply believe that some part of the human Self or Soul is not subject to the laws of space and time.'
C. G. Jung

Celebrities now talk more openly about their personal 'heavenly encounters'. I included many of their amazing stories in my book *Angels Watching Over Me.*

The more we are aware that our loved ones can visit from the afterlife, the more experiences people seem to have. Folk tell me, 'Jacky, I have read your books and now believe in life after death. I decided to ask my own relative to visit and they appeared a few days later in a dream. They just wanted to reassure me that they were safe and that they still loved me.'

Some of your deceased relatives will know you are reading this book (yes, honestly) and will understand that you may be ready to have contact yourself. With your new understanding of life after life, be prepared for your own signs from the other side.

Our physical bodies die but the spirit lives on, and this is the part of us which communicates with the living. Our deceased loved ones manipulate electrical items, flicker lights, move clockwork items like clocks and toys and appear in dreams and visions. Maybe you will be lucky enough to have an experience like this.

Thousands of my readers write and tell me about their own spirit contact. These experiences are positive and uplifting. The souls of long-lost relatives are visiting from the other side of life … and all this, without the use of a medium or psychic. Why would they contact you via a third party if they could come to you personally? The more we understand the phenomenon, the safer it is for them to reach out to us.

Our loved ones visit to bring joy and comfort but they don't want to frighten us. Wonderful, isn't it?

WHAT DO THEY 'LOOK' LIKE?

Your afterlife experiences fall into different 'categories'. Sometimes our loved ones appear to look as they did when they were alive; more often they look younger, in their prime of life. Others experience a voice or a feeling that their loved one is around them – this might include their loved one touching them in some way (a hand on the shoulder or a comforting hand in your hand, for example).

Let's have a look at some of your great questions.

WHY DO THEY VISIT?

What's the purpose of these 'close encounters'?

Dear Jacky

I lost my mother last year. We weren't particularly close when she was alive but about eight months after she passed I had a strange dream about her. I was in a supermarket with my shopping trolley and then she passed me with her own shopping trolley. I said hello when I recognized her.

After a few moments it occurred to me that she was dead and I called her back to ask her how she was. She just smiled and told me she loved me, and then I woke up.

The strange thing was that she looked so well, younger even. Why did she visit me? Was this even real? It certainly felt real.
Sam, France

Dear Sam
What a great question. Yes, in my opinion this was a real visit from your mother in spirit. It is common to dream of the deceased, but spirit visitation is different and there are several pointers that show this difference. Here are the indicators which appeared in your dream:

1. You realized in the 'dream' that your mother had died and therefore were surprised to see her (you were lucid and aware).
2. She looked younger and 'well' (spirit can show themselves in any way they want to, but usually choose to show themselves to us in a way that shows them 'at their best').
3. Your mother took you to a normal and safe environment (the supermarket). This makes the visit feel casual and acceptable.
4. Your mother's message was a common one: 'I love you.' It seems likely that she realized that when she was living she had not expressed this to you (you told me that you were not close

when your mother was alive). I am sure she was making up for lost time.

5. It is common to wake up right after a spirit encounter – it helps you to remember your special 'gift' from the other side.

Jacky

There are many other reasons why our loved ones might visit us from the other side of life. Here are a few more that I have discovered:

- They want to let us know they arrived safely in heaven.
- They might be apologizing for something they did wrong in life – or think they did wrong.
- Our loved ones like to let us know that they are aware of the important times in our lives (births, marriages, awards we have received, etc.) and that they are proud of us.
- Sometimes they come to visit our new partners, and visit new babies.
- They like to protect us and offer us warnings in dangerous situations.
- Often our loved ones like to let us know that we are not alone – that we are being helped by those on the other side.
- They want to tell us that they are proud of us.

Dream visits are very common and there are many more stories like this one to come.

NO REGRETS

Hi Jacky

I really enjoyed reading your story in *Woman's Own* magazine. I have also visited your website and found this very interesting, too.

I've had a particularly difficult time over the past few years. My lovely mum died and, regrettably, I didn't get to say goodbye to her. This has caused me a lot of guilt and heartache.

My marriage has also broken down due to my husband's infidelity and I am on my own with two young children.

I would very much like to know about my guardian angel. Is there really someone looking out for me? How will I know? I feel very alone just now, and a bit of hope for the future would be lovely.

Best wishes,

Shona, England

Hello, Shona

I am so sorry that you lost your lovely mum, but please do not worry for a second longer about it. Many people wait to be alone to die, and families can sit round the bedside for weeks but the moment they pop out for cup of coffee, their loved one passes over. We can't possibly get to say 'goodbye' to every single relative. It's just not achievable, but of course it is not 'goodbye' but rather, as the French say, 'au revoir'; because once we too return to spirit we will all meet again.

I feel sure you will find my book *Angels Watching Over Me* very useful. My book explains more about grief, death and dying – but in a positive and uplifting way. The book is full of suggestions about how to honour your loved ones, and has information about traditional ways to communicate with the other side of life – it's a real 'how to' guide and is popular with those of my readers who work in the health professions.

Millions see their passed-over relatives 'in spirit' in the hours and days before and after they die. Many times a loved one (perhaps lying in a coma) will be free of the body and float to living family members to say goodbye. This is especially common with children, who are particularly receptive to spirit contact.

A great party is held in heaven when the soul returns. Some people get a glimpse of this. After my own dad passed he showed my sisters and me a glimpse of his own reunion. During a dream visitation we were able to witness as Dad was greeted by queues of his own deceased relatives and friends. One day ... when it is 'our time', we will experience the same thing ... but in the meantime it's important that you live your best life right now.

It must be a challenge to be a single parent at this time and this will add to your stress, but please believe me when I say that you do have a guardian angel and I also hear the name BETH for you. If you want to connect more with your angel, try meditation. This relaxed bodily state will make it easier to reach out to your spiritual helpers.

Take care.

Jacky

Not having had a chance to say goodbye is a common worry. Many stories in my files show loved ones coming back to say 'goodbye' in dreams and visions because it has not been possible for them to say goodbye in the hours and days before they passed.

The dying often make this choice on purpose. It makes it easier for them to let go of the physical body without relatives and friends who are willing them to live! In many ways it can be less stressful than watching a person take their final breath. Whatever way you look at it, it's simply not possible to be with every single person you love during their final moments. I wrote *Angels Watching Over Me* to address some of these worries, and often recommend the book for cases such as this one because it explains far more than a single letter of reply can do.

Our loved ones are able to tune in to our thoughts and are sympathetic to our feelings over this. Their messages are always that we should have no regrets and that, like that old saying, 'What will be will be.' Our loved ones want us to be happy and to continue to live a happy life on 'this side' of life.

SAFELY IN HEAVEN ... OR NOT?

Luckily, this sort of dream visitation is very rare.

Dear Angel Lady

I'm not certain you can help, but it's well worth the try. I'm concerned that a friend of mine hasn't quite made it to heaven. He's only recently passed over and his girlfriend told me she'd had a dream about him. In the dream, she'd had to tell him he was dead and that she was arranging his funeral! He only replied, 'Oh' before she woke up.

I've asked my angels (in a letter kept under my pillow) if they could let me know he got there safely. Is this something they can answer for me? Is there a special way I should write my request to them? It bothers me that he had to be told he'd died, though I've considered it could have been her state of mind playing tricks on her.

Any advice would be very gratefully received. Many thanks for your time, Angel Lady.
Joanna, Scotland

Hi Joanna
If the death is sudden or the passing was done 'unconsciously', then I believe there can be a few days' delay in our loved ones realizing they are dead. This happens more when the death is unexpected (during war, for example, when one minute the person is alive and the next they are gone).

The fact that when they visit we are 'aware' that they are dead is what makes these experiences 'visitations' rather than ordinary dreams, so it's not anything to do with your friend's state of mind. This is a real spirit contact. Sometimes our loved ones can visit even in the hours after their passing. Even though they have made it safely to heaven, they are able to come back and say hi.

It's actually common to be confused when a loved one appears in these very real contacts. We, the dreamer, will ask, 'Why are you here? You're dead, aren't you?' Usually the deceased will say, 'No, I'm fine ... look.' They may not be confused but trying to reassure us that they really are 'alive' (... albeit in another dimension).

There are no particular wrong or right ways of asking the angels to help with any situation – the most important thing is that you do ask. No doubt you will get your sign that he has arrived safely as soon as it is possible for him to do so.

In this case I do not feel you have anything to worry about. He certainly knows he is dead now anyway. Of course there are many who will believe this is just a dream, but in the circumstances your friend would be the best judge. I personally believe this falls into the visitation category – it's real.

Best wishes,

Jacky

Sometimes a passing can be so quick or so peaceful that the deceased really is unaware that he or she has died right away; this is true in those cases where it's a 'perfect death' where we just slip away quietly. Don't panic!

Angels, spirit guides and other loved ones are on hand to collect the dying and so they don't normally have long to wait. There are many stories of the dying actually seeing these previously deceased friends and relatives in the hours and days before their passing. Sometimes these afterlife visitors are even witnessed by others in the room, so we know that this is true. Nurses, doctors and hospice workers have extraordinary and heart-warming stories to tell of angels appearing during a patient's final moments.

STILL SUPPORTING YOU

Dear Jacky

My grandfather passed 37 years ago this month. A few months after he passed away I discovered I was pregnant with my first child. For a while, when I was about six months pregnant, I became really frightened about the birth. Then one night I had a dream. Well, I was asleep at the time, but it was so vivid that to this day I still remember every detail, so I don't think it was a normal dream.

I was standing in the road outside Granddad's house at night, under the street light, with Granddad. He told me not to be scared, everything would be fine and I would have a lovely baby girl. From that moment on my fear disappeared and I was so convinced I would have a girl that I started buying pink baby clothes. (There were no scans in those days!) My daughter was born a year almost to the day after Granddad passed … so he was right, it was a girl.

My other visitation concerns my lovely dad. He passed just over six years ago. A few days after his funeral I had another of 'those dreams', again very vivid. I dreamt I was in the shop where I worked when Dad walked through the door. He was looking very well, and much younger. He asked me why everyone was sad, so I told him 'Because you died.' He replied, 'No, I didn't, I'm fine, look at me!'

Best wishes,

Caroline, England

Hi Caroline

Thank you so much for sharing this with me. Your stories are 'classic' visitation stories and, as you suggest, don't sound like normal dreams to me at all. I love that Dad and Granddad both came back in different ways … at different times, to reassure you. Isn't it wonderful that they were able to do that?

In these 'dream' visitations, we always know that our loved ones are dead. Their goal is to show us that they are still alive on some level, and this seems to be exactly what you experienced.

Thank you again for sharing your experiences with me. I am glad you were comforted by them, as was their intention.

Jacky

WORRIED ABOUT THE MESSAGE RECEIVED

Many people receive these visits from loved ones after they pass over but their messages are not always as clear as

Caroline's were. Sadly this causes a little worry about what the message might be, but there is usually no need to worry at all. Shauna and I exchanged several emails.

Dear Angel Lady

I am writing to you because I need help in understanding what my dead father's message means to me. You see, yesterday I had a near-death experience.

The night before I'd had a really painful headache right behind my eye. Once I was able to fall asleep I was awoken about five hours later by the 'grim reaper' who had one huge skeleton hand all the way around my head squeezing it very hard. I woke up screaming and my husband Steve calmed me down, telling me it was just a nightmare, which I was all too willing to believe. Then I went into the bathroom, but once in there I blacked out and fell and hit my head hard on the bathtub. I was knocked out and not breathing. Steve did CPR and called 999. I was then taken to the hospital.

I woke up, but my memory was confused. I was back in time to when I had my last child, 17 years ago. I was very upset that they would not let me near the baby. I wanted to see my ex-husband Bill, whom I had divorced years ago, and my mother and father – my father died 15 years ago. They tried to bring my husband Steve in but I thought he was the grim reaper.

Now I tell you all this because this is how it was told to me; I have no memory of what happened at this time. The next thing that I do remember very clearly is that, just after they tried to bring Steve to me, my father came to me in a vision, looking like he had 15 years ago. I didn't remember that he was dead. I gripped his hand and then hugged him for dear life; I could smell his cologne that he always wore.

He told me this: 'Just be good and everything will be alright.' I told him I would and he got up and left the room. Then my husband Steve came in the room and I knew who he was, but it hit me hard that my father was really dead and I had just talked to him.

My question is, what did my dad mean by saying, 'Just be good and everything will be alright'? What is good to one person is wrong to another, isn't it? What do you think of all this? I told my mother all about it and she said that she sees my dad all the time. I am so stressed over all this and really don't know what I can tell people without them thinking I am crazy.

Please help me!

Shauna

Hello, my love

You really sound like you have been through the mill – no wonder you are confused!

I can't explain why you might have seen a 'grim reaper' – the angel of death (as the crossing-over angel is called) is a gentle and loving being and people who have near-death experiences never usually want to remain in our world but can't wait to return to life on the 'other side', what is seen as our real home. Your vision of a grim reaper could have been caused by all the pain and confusion you were going through – a sort of hallucination.

Another explanation is that your brain, in its traumatized state, has connected you momentarily to a negative energy or the lower astral realms (your spiritual self should NOT have been there!).

OK, now, the visit from your dad. That WAS real and is called a spirit visitation. I have had hundreds of accounts just like yours.

Do not agonize over the message. Parents tell their children to 'be good' all the time but all they mean is 'Be quiet … be calm … ' (so he was saying relax, don't fight the doctors and nurses because you're going to be fine).

Here are some common messages from those in heaven:

- Don't worry, I am OK.
- I still love you and will never leave you (I am still here for you).
- Love is the answer to everything, only love is real.
- Be good, be nice to each other, spend more time with other people.
- Our earthly life is only temporary and soon we will all be together again in heaven.
- Have more fun and take life less seriously.

... and variations on the above! Your dad only means – be the best that you can be. His message is 'shorthand' for all the messages above. How amazing that you had the opportunity to see your dad, and at a time when you needed his comfort. I hope your body has healed.

Take care.

Jacky

Shortly afterwards I received a wonderful reply. Letters like these remind me of why I love my job!

Hi Jacky
Thank you from the bottom of my heart for replying to me. You have helped me in ways that you will never know. I will look for your next book with great joy.

Thanks again.
Love, Shauna

Thanks, Shauna! When we have these experiences they can be very profound and life-changing. The biggest problem is usually finding someone to discuss the experience with – as we would do with other things that happen to us in our lives.

This does seem to be a growing phenomenon and so the more information that becomes available for us to study, the less frightening it will seem. If you want others to learn more about the phenomenon, lend them your copy of this book! (Make sure they give it back!)

PRAYERS TO OUR LOVED ONES ON THE OTHER SIDE OF LIFE

Dear Jacky
When we pray to our loved ones, do they hear us?

Thanks for your time and cooperation.
Liz, USA

Hello, Liz

Prayer is a powerful tool of communication. Our energy when combined with others' is particularly strong and effective. People who are unconscious and those who've had near-death experiences have even heard others' prayers for them.

Prayer seems to reach through these higher states of consciousness (which is another way of explaining death from the physical realm). So I would have to say YES for sure!

Jacky x

A LITTLE MORE ON FEATHER SIGNS

Feathers can be associated with the spirit of our loved ones as well as with the appearance of a guardian angel. I receive a lot of correspondence on this subject.

Dear Jacky

Some time ago I heard that if you found a feather lying on the ground in your garden or near your house it meant that a loved one in the guise of an angel had visited you, or wanted to reassure you. What are your feelings about this?

Since my dear mother passed away three years ago, I have found numerous feathers, mainly white, in my garden, especially near the roses that she planted. Her ashes and those of my father were scattered over the rose beds (at their request), and I always feel comforted around that area. I also saw a pure white dove sitting near the roses the day we scattered Mum's ashes. He stayed for a while and didn't seem to be afraid of us at all. Do you think I may be imagining this because I want to believe in it?

Sincerely,

Diane

Hi Diane

I am sure there is truth in this. Feathers do appear in the most unlikely places sometimes, and I feel this is often (although not always) a result of spirit answering our prayers for confirmation that they are with us.

Our ancestors believed that angels were a type of bird, or sometimes believed that angels had wings (to enable them to fly), so this would account for the belief in the connection between angels and feathers in the first place. If you are getting a lot of feathers around the rose bushes, then it could well be a sign. The important thing is that the feathers have meaning … for you.

Ask your own angels to bring you a feather in a place where one would not be expected and see what happens.

Best wishes,

Jacky

It is hard for me to say specifically if individual feathers are signs from loved ones. Sometimes I get a sense of it, or feel a message from a loved one when people write to me, but normally I don't. As with all of these things it can be down to personal interpretation or that 'gut instinct' again. I always ask people, 'What do *you* think? Is it a sign?' Usually people just 'know'.

LOSS OF A PET

Continuing our feather theme, people occasionally find feathers after losing pets just as they do after losing a loved one. Anna had written to me several times when she shared this story. Was this a sign from the angels that her dog had arrived safely in doggie heaven?

Dear Jacky

When my first dog died (the one who had been in a car accident with me), I was extremely distressed. It hit me much harder than I thought it would and I missed her so much, and still do even though I now have two other much-loved dogs.

One evening, about three days afterwards, I was sitting crying on my back doorstep and a pure white feather floated down and landed on the path right in front of me. I have never seen a white feather in the garden before or since, and I knew straight away that it was a sign from her that she was OK where she was and wasn't far away.

I have told my sister to visit your website ... she is another great believer in angels!

Best wishes and thanks for your interest.

Anna

Hi Anna

Ah yes – the classic white feather! It is becoming more and more used by the angels – almost like a universal symbol! Many people collect these special feathers and tuck them in to their bag or pocket, or stick them in the side of photograph frames – especially those containing photographs of loved ones both alive and deceased.

I miss my pets, too, and it is hard to get over losing a special being in our lives ... people or our furry friends.

Just knowing they are waiting on the other side is a comfort to us. Many people even write to me with stories of their pets returning to them in special ways (feeling their dog brush against their legs, or their spirit-cats padding up and down on the bed!). It all helps to ease the grief. I have included sections about animal afterlife stories in many of my other books and you might enjoy reading these.

Take care and thank you for sharing your story.

Jacky

This story is particularly sad but it does show how important pets are in our lives.

Dear Jacky

On Wednesday 4th February at around 7 a.m. my children's pet cat died very suddenly with no history of illness. She was only around two years old and it was most distressing for my children. It was my son's birthday on this date and he was actually holding her at the time she was dying, while the other two children and I watched helplessly.

My oldest has had bad dreams about the cat since she died. We are used to animals dying because my husband has a farm, but this was very distressing. I just want to know how she died so suddenly and what can have happened to her. Then I can let go of her.

Yours faithfully,

Cath, Cyprus

Hi Cath

I am so sorry for the loss of your cat – well, kitten, really, as she was so young. I am sure it was a very distressing moment for you all. The only way you can tell for sure how or why your pet died is to have a post-mortem (your vet may be prepared to do this). It could have been caused by many different things. Also, as with humans, sometimes our pets' lives are short and sometimes long.

I am sure your son's bad dreams are related to the shock of losing his pet, rather than being something spiritual. After losing a loved one (person or pet), our children's biggest worry usually is that others around them will die, too. Time, love and lots of reassurance will help.

Although I can't tell you why she died, I can reassure you that pets have souls and go to heaven in the same way that human souls do. Many have experiences of their pets reaching out from heaven (my own dog appeared in several dreams after she passed over).

In many of my books I have shared some of the wonderful stories of afterlife contact – our pets don't 'talk' to us (as they didn't do this in life) but they communicate in a telepathic way and let us know that they made it safely to their new heavenly homes, and thank us for loving them while they were in their Earth-body.

By asking for our pets to appear in (nice) dreams, many have experienced success with this technique. In the meantime, may I suggest you make a memorial book in which you can all write favourite memories, draw pictures of your cat and paste in other cat pictures? Maybe your children could draw or paint some of her favourite things and add this, too? This will help the family to remember some of the happy times rather than being left with the overriding memory of the sadness of her death.

For more suggestions of after-death rituals, may I recommend my book *Angels Watching Over Me* (you may be able to borrow this from your local library)?
Jacky

NOT SO NICE VISITS

Although most spirit visits are nice ones, just occasionally they are not. The experience here clearly shows a normal 'nightmare' type of dream which sometimes follows a trauma or stressful experience.

Dear Jacky
I hope you can help me. At night I am woken up by people in my room. Then they vanish. Sometimes they appear in colour, and sometimes they are in black and white.

My husband sleeps on my left, but I sense someone on my right. Are these dreams or am I going mad? A woman told me they are echoes of vibration. I see these things even when I'm away from home. This has been going on for nearly 13 years now.

Thank you, I hope you can put my mind at rest.

Margaret, Ireland

Dear Margaret

You are clearly very 'sensitive' (some would even call you 'a Sensitive' or a medium) to these things as you have been picking up spirit energy for a long time. I think I understand what your friend meant about the echoes. There are several types of energy that we can experience:

- Spirit energy which is aware and wants to interact (mainly our own loving relatives who want to reassure us).
- Spirits of the deceased who may have lived in the house or be attached to it in some way (they may not even know that we exist most of the time; they are just visiting their old home).
- 'Energy memory' or echoes, as your friend calls them. These are your classic 'ghosts' in that they are simply a recording on the atmosphere (held within the fabric of the building). Imagine

how a voice is recorded on magnetic tape – this is a similar thing.

- You might also be experiencing your own guardian angel or spirit guide – and your fear is what is translating this positive experience into a negative one.

If you are at all worried, you can 'smudge' your bedroom. You can buy bundles of dried white 'sacred sage' on the internet and from specialist shops. You light the end of the smudge (or smudging wand as it is sometimes called), then blow it out and waft the smoke around the room – right into the corners and even under the bed (be very careful not to set fire to anything). This makes it more difficult for negative (scary) visitors to appear.

For more information about clearing negative energies (and spirits), you might enjoy my book *Angel Kids*.

Let me know how you get on.

Jacky

Chapter 7

Your Afterlife Stories

'We have no reliable guarantee that the afterlife will be any less exasperating than this one, have we?'
Noel Coward

I know you will enjoy these wonderful stories of communication from the other side of life.

RINGING ON THE DOOR

'My brother passed away five years ago. We were very close. About a year after he had passed away, I fitted a cordless doorbell to my door. Well, after about a month the doorbell would ring at all times of the day and night. Whenever I went to check, no one would be there.

'One day I had just let someone out of the front door and immediately the doorbell rang. Ha! I thought, got you now, and I immediately opened the door again – but lo and behold, no one was there. As I stood there the doorbell began to ring. I stood mesmerized as I wasn't touching it but it was ringing. My husband came to see what I was playing at. 'It's not me,' I said and he stood there also in shock as the doorbell continued to ring.

'Well, after that someone broke the bell button downstairs so you couldn't push it, and I removed it but left the base upstairs on the wall. A few months after that, the doorbell began to ring again. I wasn't frightened, but somehow knew it was my brother communicating, just to let me know he was there. In a way it was quite comforting.

'About five months ago, after about two years without a "ring", the doorbell rang. My elder son was at the house and he looked shocked. I knew it was my brother but wondered why he'd rung. Anyway, before I went to sleep that night I asked him that, if it was him, to come to me in my sleep and let me know what he wanted.

'At 1.18 a.m. the doorbell woke up the whole household with its continual ringing! I had to get up and take it down to stop it. When I woke up the following morning, I just laughed to myself as I knew it was my brother playing games. When I said for him to come to me, I meant in a dream, but he was always the joker and decided to do it his way.

'Even now when I think about it, I can just see him laughing at the funny joke he played on me. This is not the only time he's "visited" me. He often gives me hugs and I know when he's around me. I will always miss him, but I know he's only a heartbeat away. (God bless you, Phil. Love you.) – *Jane, England*

A while later, Jane was kind enough to share another experience with me.

I MISS YOU

'I was sleeping and my dream took me to a village hall where there seemed to be a party going on. As I walked into the hall, my eyes were drawn to the stage at the end of the hall, and standing there leaning on the stage was my brother Phillip. Well, my heart leapt, as I was really missing him. He looked wonderful in his jacket, white shirt and jeans (just how he used to dress) and he was smiling at me. I was so glad to see him and as he held out his arms to me I ran to him. Well, I hugged him and he hugged me, but as I hugged him my arms went right through him – but even this didn't matter because I knew he was spirit. It didn't take away the feeling of love his hug gave me.

The hug was wonderful. Phil said, "I've missed you." I asked him if he was happy with the way we did his funeral.

"Oh yes," he said. Then we had a good laugh talking about some of the people who were there.

'It was so good to see him again. We chatted for a while, then he had to go. When I awoke in the morning, I felt so humble, so full of love and so at peace. I draw on that feeling when I'm at a low ebb or when the feeing of loss shows itself, and it gives me comfort. I know he's looking out for me and will never leave me.' – *Jane, England*

ROSARY SIGN

'I lost my granny very suddenly five months ago. It was a massive shock as we'd just seen each other the previous week while we were visiting family in South Uist. Granny was quite young. She was like my second mum, so it was very traumatic.

About two months later I had what I think could have been a dream visitation. In the "dream", my mum was having a party and I had come downstairs with my mum and two of her friends to say goodbye to another friend.

'As I turned around, my granny was standing in the porch. I could only see the top half of her body but she was wearing a recognizable coat. She looked younger and had a massive smile on her face. I immediately ran up to her, crying as she opened her arms.

'She didn't say anything but I was telling her how much I loved her and missed her. She felt solid, warm and real, and it was the most powerful thing I have ever experienced. I also remember feeling as if everything around us had disappeared and we were now in an open white space and were glowing a golden light. Then I woke but I really felt like I had been hugged, and I had real tears on my face.

'I also have another story about my granny. At Christmas we went to South Uist to spend the holiday with my grandpa. Christmas had been my granny's favourite day of the year so it was a very hard without her, so I decided to ask my granny for a sign to let me know she was OK.

'While we were away, one of my granny's work colleagues gave me a present. This woman's mum had been good friends with my granny and they were recently at the ceremony of the 50th anniversary of the Lady of the Isles statue in South Uist together. This woman also had a visit from Granny in a dream. Granny told her that they would still be going to events together – although Granny was going as a ghost!

Granny's friend went to another event and the woman picked up a pearl rosary bracelet as a gift for me. I believe this was my sign, as it was like a Christmas present from my granny. She'd given me a pearl rosary necklace for my First Communion, and this bracelet matched!

'Even though Granny is in the afterlife, she still managed to give me a Christmas present! Funny how that worked out!' – *Katie, Scotland*

MY GRANDDAD SEES DEAD PEOPLE

'I have a 96-year-old granddad who, I might add, is very much "with it"! Three years ago he lost his wife. She had an aneurism which she lived with for a couple of years, until one day, after a lovely day out shopping together, she collapsed. Granddad's life changed from that day on.

'Granddad is the most cynical person I know. He says "When you're dead, you're dead" and he has never been interested in hearing anything to the contrary.

'Then something strange happened. A few months back I was stunned with what he felt he needed to tell me. He didn't think anybody would believe him, so he kept it under his hat for a while, but he was so intrigued with what he saw, he felt compelled to share his experience ...

'Granddad said he was sitting in his usual chair at home watching the TV, when all of a sudden, all these people appeared from behind his chair, all walking past him in a long line. There were hundreds of them! They were walking along their own path on a different level. One particular little boy walked past and turned around to say hello to Granddad. Granddad said the little boy's mother grabbed him and told him, "Stop bothering the man."

'Granddad couldn't quite take in what was going on in his own lounge, so he got up out of his chair and opened the door. All these people were still following each other across the hallway and through the next room, until they disappeared. Here's what happened next! Standing in the downstairs toilet, Grandad suddenly realized there was a man standing right next to him! "What do you think you're doing?" he demanded, but the man just smiled. Then Granddad decided to retire to bed.

'He told me he was getting himself undressed in his bedroom when suddenly a man appeared again, leaving him feeling quite embarrassed! Granddad said he tried to talk to the man, but he disappeared. He felt there was never a time when he was frightened or uneasy, but his story made the rest of the family slightly worried. We thought maybe all these people had come to take him away.

'Since that time Grandad has not experienced anything more. I believe everything he has told me. There is no way on Earth that he could possibly have made any of this up.'
– *Sally, England*

THE HOUSE OF MANY VISITORS

'My husband and I moved into our house some 15 years ago. It's a very friendly and warm terraced house and around 100 years old.

'We had our first child, Jack, in 1992, and when he was about three years old he used to see a "man at the window" (his words) at the end of our lounge facing our back garden.

'For a long period Jack would see this man and he was a little frightened by him. I actually never saw this man, neither did I sense his presence. I once asked Jack to ask the man his name, and Jack told me the spirit was a friend and described an old man. Then he never mentioned him again.

'We had our second son, Joe, in 1996. Strangely, when he was around three, maybe three and a half, he started seeing a man in exactly the same place. (Please note, though, that neither son knew that the other had had this experience.) This time, however, Joe used to go to the window and speak to the man. Joe was never frightened and seemed to feel drawn to the man, and often spoke to him.

'At the time it really unnerved me, and in the end I told Joe to tell the man to go away. He did. Neither of the boys saw him for many years.

'About five years ago a friend came to my house one evening and brought someone with her. I'd just been upstairs and walked into the lounge and my friend's companion asked me if I knew there was a spirit here in my house. (This woman didn't know me, neither did she or my friend know anything about my boys' experiences.) She told me that she'd seen the spirit of an old man, and it was in the exact same place where the boys had seen the spirit. She told me he was not a relative and he meant no harm. It was confirmation to me that it was all real anyway.

'Jack is now 11 and we've both had various experiences in the house. I would often smell the aroma of pipe tobacco, and once I woke up and felt something touch my face very gently … like the stroke of a feather. Another time I was sitting in my room and I felt a touch along my arm. I did ask whoever it was not to do that as I didn't like it much! And it stopped.

'On another occasion I woke up to see a dark shadow of a person stooping at the foot of my bed! Maybe this is the same person who messes with the electrics in the house?

'For example, I have a vacuum cleaner which has a knob that controls the suction and on a few occasions the suction kept going from maximum to minimum. Every time I would turn it back to maximum, it would switch itself back to minimum! I found this quite comical and just thought someone was playing games with me!

'In another instance, the pull cord that turns on our electric shower would come on by itself. I would notice the 'on' light and pull the cord to switch it off. Bear in mind that I was the only person in the house at the time. The next time I'd go into the bathroom, the 'on' light would be on again!! The only way to operate it is by actually tugging on the pull cord!

'My mum has been touched on the back in our kitchen, too. Sometimes when I'm taking my make-up off in the bathroom I can feel a presence, as if someone is there watching me.

'Three years ago I was shopping in our local supermarket and stopped to say hello to a woman that lives just down the road from me. She told me that she used to live in our house when she was a little girl, and that before then the house had belonged to her grandparents. (Her grandfather was the first person to have lived in our house.) I took the opportunity of sharing some of our experiences, and she was very interested in what I told her. She then went on to explain that her grandfather used to smoke a pipe, and I wondered immediately if her grandfather was our mystery spirit! Perhaps he was hoping for my encounter with his granddaughter so I could let her know he was OK.

'Last year the activity really peaked. Jack's bedroom is right next to the bathroom and he started to feel uneasy when he was in his room playing on his computer. It got to the point where he was really scared and just would not go upstairs on his own. One day he came running down the stairs in floods of tears and told me that he felt someone watching him from behind and actually breathing down his neck. He was so upset, bless him.

'I mentioned all this to a clairvoyant friend of mine. She advised me to light a candle and just tell the spirit that he was making my son very upset and uncomfortable and to tell him it was time to move on to his special place. Well, I did that in a kind and friendly way … especially as we thought the visitor might be my neighbour's granddad.

'After that the spirit did "move on", but funnily enough I missed him! His absence was so conspicuous. I often tried to feel if he was around, but he'd gone.' – *Julie, UK*

If your children are disturbed by spirit activity, you'll find lots of advice in my book *Angel Kids,* published by Hay House.

SOMEWHERE OVER THE RAINBOW

'My dad passed suddenly last January. It was not expected and it left us devastated. Over the next few days we were arranging his funeral and were deciding what music we were going to play in the crematorium. Eventually we decided on "Somewhere over the Rainbow" (that's where I like to think he is now).

'On the morning of his funeral the sun was shining and we were all really upset and dreading the day ahead of us. No one really wanted this to be the day we were to say our final farewells. I had just popped outside to get something from the car, when out of nowhere, at the bottom of our street I spotted a rainbow. It was the brightest rainbow I had ever seen. I ran back inside to fetch my mother and when she came outside she couldn't believe what she was seeing either; there was no rain to be seen anywhere.

'I rang my sister who lives just a few minutes away to tell her, and she too was really shocked … it was perfect. I am sure this was a sign from my dad to let us know he was with us that day and that he was walking by our side, guiding us through the day.

'We have experienced our rainbows a few times since, on the days that are really stressful and we're feeling really down. That's when the beautiful rainbows have appeared and my heart feels lifted, just as if I'd had a hug from my dad. All of the family feels as if this is my dad's "call-sign".

'I also ask my angels to bring Dad to visit me in my dreams, and I feel really lucky because this has happened twice so far. I just wanted to see him and to ask him if he is OK.

'One night I said "Dad, are you OK?" and he replied he was fine and excitedly told me he didn't need his wheelchair any more. "That's all I needed to know," I replied.

Not long after my dad had died, my mam was doing some weeding in the garden and my son, who was five at the time, was jumping about in the garden. Out of the blue he said to Mam, "Nana, Granddad said he's sorry that he is not here, but he is OK."

'It made the hairs stand up on the back of my mam's neck. My son wouldn't normally say something like that, and when Mam asked him where Granddad was, he replied, "He's standing on the path next to you."

'A few months later Dad visited again. My son said he had seen Granddad waving to him out of the clouds!

'I know my dad is with us always, he would never be far away.' – *Linsey, England*

HELLO FROM A CINEMA IN HEAVEN

'I took your book *An Angel by My Side* on holiday with me to Greece in August '07. It was recommended by a friend of mine who had recently lost her mum. She told me she'd found your book comforting.

'I have always believed that our loved ones go on ahead of us to a better place until we join them, and over the years I've had some strange "happenings". It was not until I read your book that I realized my mum had contacted me shortly after her death (13 years ago), but I just hadn't realized it. Here's my story.

'I had the most "vivid" dream one night. It was about six months after my mum had passed away. In the dream I was in the foyer of a cinema and one of the attendants working there was a woman I knew named Sylvia (she used to be our cleaner at work).

'Sylvia approached me as I walked in and said, "Oh, Lorraine, I'm glad you're here, I have someone who wants to see you." Feeling intrigued, I walked with her to the doors of the cinema (where you would go through to view a film). When the doors opened, instead of seating there were lots of people sitting around square tables in a massive room with dull lighting. All the people seated were elderly and they were all chatting to each other.

'Sylvia guided me down towards the front of the room and said to me, "There, look to your left and you will see someone you know." I looked and there was Mum, and she was sitting in a wheelchair (she had been in a wheelchair for seven years due to a massive stroke at the age of 69). She was talking to a man sitting at her table. My heart leapt and I immediately called out to her and ran over to her. Mum heard me call her and she turned around and began crying. We hugged each other for ages and we both continued crying for what seemed like ages and ages.

'Mum held my face in her hands and kept repeating over and over again, "Oh, my darling, I have been looking for you everywhere, where have you been?"

'After we dried our tears I sat with her and she told me she was fine, she was happy. She let me know that she is with lots of old friends and they talk about the "good old days".

'She told me that I would always be successful in my life and that she loved me and would always be by my side. She let me know that she was so very proud of her grandsons, my two boys. Then suddenly Mum said to me, "I have to go now, darling." I cried again and begged her not to go, but she had no choice. I was transported back through the doors of the cinema into the foyer area and this is when I woke up.

'Over the years this experience has never faded.' – *Lorraine, England*

PARTY CAKES

'My daughter Hayley and I were home alone. She was in her room playing and I'd been cleaning up when I looked into her room to see what she was up to. I found she had taken all her toys out and was setting them up for a tea party.

'I went out quietly, and secretly made up a batch of little cakes for the party. I'd just taken some out of the oven when Hayley came in and said, "Mummy, there is a woman in my room." I hadn't heard a car pull up outside and the only way into the house was through the back door. So I asked Hayley if the woman was still there and she said yes, so I took her hand and we went back up to her room.

'The toys were all set out but the room was empty. Hayley looked so upset that the woman had gone. I told her to go get the cakes from the kitchen for the tea party and I did a quick search of the house and yard and found no one at all.

'When I went back into the bedroom I said in a firm voice, "If you want to play with Hayley you can, but you are not allowed to scare her or upset her."

'Then Hayley and I just sat down with our cake and "tea" (cordial) on the floor with the dolls.

'The woman is still around. Hayley says her name is Flo and she is my great-grandmother. It seems she has always looked after Hayley (who is now 13). Hayley still talks to spirit people all the time, and Flo (and others) are in and out of my home all the time … animals too.'

* * * *

I hope you enjoyed that wonderful selection of stories. Now let's have a look at some of your questions about spirit guides.

Chapter 8

Questions about Your Spiritual Guides

'O tribe of spirits and of men, if you are able to slip through the parameters of the skies and the Earth, then do so.'
The Koran

Often when people talk about their guardian angels they actually mean their spiritual guides. Spirit guides are souls like us, but more advanced spiritually. The role of a spirit guide is to help keep us on our chosen life path. Our guides have chosen to act as teachers and are aware of the lessons we have chosen to live through on our earthly journey.

Each of us is born with a spirit guide who follows us all the way through our lives. We also have specialist guides who pop in from time to time to help out with any special needs or lessons that we choose to learn.

Spirit guides are like guardian angels but because they have nearly always lived human lives they have a better understanding of what it is to be human.

As with our angels, most people want to know how they can contact their spirit guides and then how to work with them once they have made the connection!

WHAT IS A GUIDE?

Dear Angel Lady

My friend and I went to see a local medium a few weeks ago and she told us both that we have our own spirit guides. We were both excited at the time because she made it sound like a good thing.

Afterwards we felt a bit stupid, though, because we didn't ask her what she meant. What are spirit guides exactly and what is the point of having one?

Justin and Samantha, UK

Hi Justin and Samantha

I hope you enjoyed your trip to see the medium. I am sure the medium is correct because I believe we all have our own spiritual guides who work with us from the other side.

The spirit guide's role is to keep us on track and remind us of our goals. They give us little reminders along life's path and help us to meet the people we need to meet and be at the places that we need to be to enable us to learn our chosen lessons.

Spirit guides assist in giving us opportunities for growth. We choose certain tasks to complete before we are born, and our guides are aware of what these are (patience, tolerance and so on) ... we of course have usually forgotten (it's called the veil of illusion) ... although, surprisingly, more and more people are remembering the reasons why they have chosen their current lives.

Our guides are people whom we have known for many earthly years. They know everything about us and can access our spiritual records on the other side if they need to. These spirit records are called 'the Akashic records' or 'book of life' and record every thought, act and deed of our life (and other lives). Our guides are able to tap in to this information.

Being a guide is a very selfless act. Guides commit to supporting us during the whole of our lifetime and often through many lives. You know that, although you might not remember it at this time, your spirit guide is a very good friend indeed.
Jacky

It's true that many folk seem to be 'waking up' to who they are and why they are here. Many more people are taking an interest in their spiritual selves and considering life a great adventure and privilege.

England has many 'alternative' health and mind, body and spirit festivals. And I have been a guest speaker at lots of them. Members of the public approach me and say, 'I am here to teach people … ' or 'I know that I am helping God with healing others in need.' These people and others seem to have come to an inner knowing that there is 'more to life than this'. Our spirit guides can help us with these life goals and challenges.

CONTACTING SPIRIT GUIDES

Hello,

My name is Katrina and I am very interested in finding out how you contact your spirit guides. I meditate every evening and have done so for about four months now and still have had no contact.

I don't know what I am doing wrong. I have been told that I have the potential for being a medium by others, and some have told me that my guide is an Egyptian woman. But I still cannot seem to make contact with her.

Where I live there is nothing to help you progress spiritually. You're basically on your own. I would be so grateful if you could help me.
Katrina, Australia

Hi Katrina
Our spirit guides act in subtle ways, like angels, and you are likely to receive your contact as inspirational thoughts and intuition rather than actual words. Their communication is telepathic (nearly always).

The thoughts sound very much like your own, except when you find you are 'arguing with yourself' frequently! That's when we know that the message is coming from our guides and not from our own mind. My guide is usually right, but of course I have to find my own way and my guides have to stand back and let me!

Ask your guides to help with specific tasks and then watch out for the 'coincidences' which help to make your path easier. Their guidance will often come as an inner knowing. I'm sure you will recall many instances when you've felt this guidance but probably missed it because you were expecting to hear actual words.
Jacky

Of course, we always make the final decision. We have the final say on what we do in our lives and how we do it. Like a mother watching over her child, ultimately we have to learn through our own mistakes or find our own way of doing things. I imagine the life of a spirit guide is a very frustrating one!

ANGELS OR SPIRIT GUIDES?

Do you know the difference? Does it matter?

Dear Angel Lady

I am very excited to have heard a name during my meditation. I feel sure that it is the name of my guardian angel. The name I heard was 'Joshua', but my friend says that there is no such angel name.

We have both searched in several books and not found the name anywhere. I am worried now that my mind might have been playing tricks on me. Could this be the name of my spirit guide? Please can you let me know?

Derek, Germany

Hello, Derek

Angels will often give us a name which we can work with, as they do not really have names which translate to our language. They are really known more by the roles they perform rather than an actual name. Their 'name' (or label) may translate more as a feeling or colour – and not what we would recognize as a name at all.

This does sound like it might be your spirit guide, though. Spirit guides are advanced human souls with free will who have decided to support us during our earthly life, and angels are light-beings who follow the will of God but in part act as protectors and guardians of humankind.

Does the energy feel positive and loving to you? If so, don't worry too much about whether your helper is an angel or a guide. In time, all will be revealed.
Jacky

People do get very concerned about the difference between angels and guides, but really it shouldn't matter too much to us. What we need to be aware of more is the energy which this presence brings to us.

Our loving angels and guides don't tell us what to do but offer us suggestions, bring alternatives to our attention and support our own choices. In emergencies they might jump in and offer a warning.

Their involvement never makes us feel uncomfortable or unhappy. They never give us commands which might involve hurting or harming others or ourselves.

WHY DO WE HAVE ANGELS AND SPIRIT GUIDES?

Angels and spirit guides do have different roles to play, but both can and do work together as required.

Dear Angel Lady

I am a Catholic and was brought up to believe in guardian angels. My grandmother used to say a prayer about angels every night when she tucked me into bed.

Now I have read that we also have spirit guides who protect us, too. Why do we need both? I mean, what is the point if angels are already looking after us?

Michael, Wales

Dear Michael

Angels' primary role is to protect us. They work with larger issues such as love and healing. Angels don't really understand our day-to-day problems such as paying household bills! Angels haven't lived human lives, so many of our human struggles are hard for them to fathom.

Spirit guides, on the other hand, have usually lived at least one human life and probably hundreds or thousands. They've literally 'been there and done that', as the saying goes!

By their working together, we have a great support team.
Jacky

HOW DO SPIRIT GUIDES COMMUNICATE WITH US?

Well, of course, we already receive messages from our spirit guides, but we don't always 'hear' them!

Many years ago I was awoken with the word 'TEST' in my ear. It was a normal-sounding female voice and I sat up immediately. I was terribly excited, thinking that this was how my spirit guides were going to communicate with me.

'Yes, I hear you,' I said.

Sadly, I never heard that female voice in that same way ever again! Like most people I guess I assumed they were going to talk right into my ear with actual words, and sadly it doesn't really work that way. As with angels, their ideas come more as thoughts to us. I know I often questioned the ideas in the early stages, but now I am more aware of when my spirit guides are making suggestions.

My husband and I laugh when a 'coincidence' occurs as a result of a request we have made from our guides. Sometimes the results from our appeal arrive so quickly that it catches us by surprise. Other times the results take a little longer, but usually that is because other people are involved in some complicated puzzle and our angels and guides seem to have to put all of the pieces into place first. It's important to be patient (hard, I know). Just remember that the more difficult requests can take a little longer.

HOW DO WE COMMUNICATE WITH SPIRIT GUIDES?

Dear Jacky

I found it so heart-warming to read your pages in *It's Fate* magazine, I felt compelled to email you to ask for some advice as someone who knows what she's talking about.

I'm sure you have lots of work in your busy schedule and also many emails like mine. The reason that I write to you is to ask you if you could help me to contact my guides.

Sometimes I feel that I try too hard to achieve contact with them and end up burning myself out. I've always asked for guidance when I've needed it and I know that they're there because they've helped me before. I just wish I could have a much more advanced relationship with them like so many other mediums do. I would love to be able to have the conversations and spiritual contact with the guides, to help comfort others. Is this possible and how can it be achieved?

Yours sincerely,

Clare, England

Dear Clare

Yes, I do get hundreds of emails – but never too many not to answer every single one (in time!). 'Snail mail' letters take quite a lot longer to reply to and I usually have a large bagful sitting by my desk at any one time, but I do welcome all letters, so thank you for writing to me.

You know, I've said it before and I'll say it again: you really can't beat meditation for creating a stronger relationship with your guides and angels. Meditating really does open up the link to the higher realms and, of course, with practice you can become more psychic, too, which is a great advantage.

If you struggle with meditating, try a guided meditation recording, which will give you 'somewhere to go' and 'something to do' while you have your eyes closed! A guided meditation CD will often have relaxation exercises built into the recording and, as a result, you will begin to memorize these techniques yourself.

The alternative is to join a meditation class or work with a friend who has meditation experience and can guide you through the exercise.
Jacky

IS MY MOTHER MY GUIDE?

Dear Jacky
I would like to know if I have a guardian angel or a spirit guide and, if I have, I would like to know what his or her name is. Could my mother be my guide (because she passed away last October), or do I have another one?

If I do have a guardian angel, how do I ask him or her for help and good luck? How will I know if my guardian angel has replied to my questions? Please reply to me as soon as possible. Thanks.
Meri, UK

Dear Meri
You most certainly have got your own guardian angel and spirit guide – I hear the name 'Jason' – and also I believe that the Archangel Raphael works with you, too.

Although your mother is not your guide as such, she is working with you on the other side. Our loved ones can offer support and guidance and, in my experience, often help us with things that they are not really supposed to (shhh, don't tell anyone!). It is not easy for them to see BOTH sides, as they ALWAYS side with us ... on every occasion!

Ask your guides to leave you clues to their answers (which usually arrive in the form of 'coincidences').

As with your angels, speak to your guides as if they were close friends and always remember to say please and thank you when making a request. You can ask your questions out loud or write them down in a special notebook. Ask your guides to bring you messages in your dreams, as my own do.

Good luck,

Jacky

I believe our loved ones help us out a lot, even when we are not aware of their presence. But you can see the difficulties they face! It is hard for them to remain objective when they are helping us, because they have no wish to see us unhappy. Our guides can stand back and see the wider picture, but our loved ones can't easily do this.

Our guides have taken on the role specifically so that they can help us to learn life lessons. Our loved ones would rush in and make sure we don't suffer, even if that suffering is for the greater long-term goals of our spirit! I think we can sometimes grow more as souls by living through some of our mistakes. No doubt Grandma would disagree!

Many people see their loved ones in dreams (see the chapter on afterlife communication for more on this). On occasion our loved ones do offer us advice (and sometimes we hear a word or two in real language – the earthly voice we recognize, telling us to slow down or take care).

Remember that if Uncle Fred was a poor judge of character when he was alive, you might not want to take his advice on your new boyfriend now he has passed over!

On the other hand, if your mother appears to warn you about something in a dream, you might want to bear it in mind when making your decision. As with spirit guide help and guidance, remember that YOU always have the final decision on what is right for you in your life.

SPIRIT GUIDES COME TO COMFORT US

Dear Angel Lady

My daughter has been very depressed over the past few months due to a breakdown in a relationship; she has been getting worse recently. Over the past few weeks she has only been getting up to go to work and at the weekends she has stayed in bed drinking, just to sleep and pass the time. I have been so worried about her and one day last week I prayed (well, begged) for someone to help her.

The following day she told me something amazing had happened. She was very restless and got up at 2.10 a.m., then went back to bed and lay with her eyes closed, trying to get back to sleep. It was then that she felt someone touch her hand. She thought she could see someone in the bedroom and, as she tried to focus, she saw several people dressed in normal clothes. One of the people said to her, 'Everything will be all right' and smiled before disappearing.

As she focused on the others, each one smiled in turn and disappeared one at a time. She hadn't been drinking at this time, and she is sure she wasn't dreaming. She says she feels much better now and appears more positive. Could you tell us what this experience was?

Yours sincerely,

Moya, Italy

Hello there,

Your request gave permission for guides to call in and comfort your daughter, that is why they did. Don't worry, your daughter is not going mad!

The phrases 'everything will be fine' and 'you're going to be OK' are common messages from our guides and angels when we are down on our luck. I image the spirit that spoke to your daughter would have been her primary guide (the one that has been with her since birth) and the others are either soul friends (who will know her from previous incarnations) or other guides that are working with her right now.

Sounds crazy? I know it is hard to work with this information as it all sounds too good to be true, but believe me, I hear these stories over and over again.

Thank you for writing and sharing your special story.

Jacky

SPIRIT GUIDES AND CHILDREN

Our spirit guides are with us from birth and many parents question why their babies seem to smile or giggle at something unseen. That is, unseen to the parent, but clearly not unseen to the baby! Young children often have what we adults call 'invisible friends' and many of these companions are spirit guides, sometimes even appearing 'as' children.

I receive a lot of letters from adults who had so called 'imaginary friends' as children. It's sad when young children are not believed, isn't it?

Hello,

When I was a baby of just a few weeks old, a woman appeared by my cot. She was dressed all in blue and my mother saw her and she was quite stunned about it. She told me that this woman was so beautiful, she still believes to this day that she was an angel.

At the time my aunt was staying, and sleeping in my mum's room (my dad was sleeping in another room). When the woman moved away from my cot she went into the room where my dad was sleeping. The year was 1941, and in 1945 my dad died. Is it possible that woman was Dad's guide?

I would love to know. Thank you for reading this.

Imogen, England

Hello, Imogen

I think it was more likely to be *your* guide. When we are babies, our souls are quite loose/fluid within the body and can move in and out in the first few weeks (these events are called OBEs or out-of-body experiences). It is possible that as a spirit you were nervous about moving fully into the body of the new baby (what you now know as YOU) and your guide just popped along to check you were OK.

Your guide may have checked on your mum as well as your dad. It takes a lot of energy for our guides to show themselves in this way. Perhaps your mother needed the reassurance that you were OK.

Either way, it's wonderful to know you are protected and watched over by your guides and, in this case at least, your family have had visual proof.

Take care.

Jacky

Now I'd like to tell you a little bit about ghosts … don't be scared!

Chapter 9

Ghosts and Other Spirits

'O Death, rock me asleep,
Bring me to quiet rest,
Let pass my weary guiltless ghost
Out of my careful breast.'
Anne Boleyn

'Ghost hunting' has become a popular pastime in the UK. We have so many ghosts in England, and hunting them down has become a favourite evening pursuit.

Seeing and experiencing a ghost has become the 'roller coaster' of psychic communication: heavy on the thrill factor but, like the fairground ride, over way too quickly. What is it that makes people want to see a spirit or ghost? Although many people are interested in the 'fear factor' as a way of being entertained, others are comforted by the fact that another life exists beyond this one.

TV ghost shows are becoming more and more popular. People are excited that there might be a life beyond this one and, although the intent of any TV show is primarily to entertain, some interesting investigations have taken place. For some, paranormal TV shows will have sparked their first interest in the afterlife, the first time many have even considered that there might be more after this physical life ends. As time goes on, most are more intrigued and less scared, which has to be a good thing.

'Ghost hunting', or searching for spirits, deserves serious scientific study and it's thrilling to see more technical equipment being used to measure phenomena like the changes in temperature which often occur when the sensation of spirit energy is felt by 'sensitives' and psychics.

ORBS

One of the common phenomena discovered on a ghost hunt is orbs. I do get a lot of people sending me photographs of orbs … although I'm not sure why (I'm certainly no expert). These balls of 'light' occur a lot on photographs taken at haunted sites and around psychic people. Even experts have differing opinions on what these orbs might be – the debate's still out! Personally I think they're a mixture of the following:

- light from nearby sources, including sunlight and torches
- light which has bounced off nearby reflective surfaces
- moisture
- insects
- spirits or angels
- glare from the flash.

Strangely, orbs have been seen over fields of crops where 'crop circles' have appeared. Some people say that they can see faces in the orb pictures, and others theorize there is some sort of intelligence behind their movement.

Some images show movement inside the circle, or what appears to be a vortex of energy in the centre of the orb! Others believe that orbs are spirits or angels ... we just don't know.

LIGHT FLARES

More fascinating to me are the flashes of light which appear on photographic images which look like words, numbers or shapes – sometimes repeated on the image several times.

One photograph, which someone sent me of a wedding, contained about 10 'angel shapes' – the same exact shape appearing over and over again on the photograph. Yet strangely the photographs taken immediately before and after the image did not have the angel lights on them!

Another flare picture contained three '3s' staggered just out of alignment over the head of a young boy. Yet another reader sent me a photograph taken of 'angel bears' (Christmas decorations) after they had been arranged on a door. Light flares appear over almost the entire photograph – in the shape of a giant angel!

NOT AN ANGEL?

Dear Jacky

I have been looking at your website. It was really informative and impressive, until I got to the children's photos bit (the children with the strange lights around them in a photograph). If I weren't a believer already, and someone who already works with spirit guides, I think these photos would have had me doubting the whole thing. I'm not a photographer, but those bits of light, etc. on the photos could have been anything, and it would appear to be no more than wishful thinking by people to suggest that they are angels or spirits.

I wouldn't want other people to see the photographs and then decide the whole angels/spirit guide thing is rubbish … Just some feedback for you, anyway.

Regards,

James, England

In my reply I actually agreed with James! The photographs on my website are there for fun only, and it's important to look at these images objectively and not get too excited. Sometimes a blob of light on an image is just that, a blob of light! Many suggestions include reflections, insects and flashes from the camera. Of course, if you suggest that all of these images are explainable, that is also unfair. Sometimes we'll just never know! Keep an open mind and decide for yourself.

STRANGE MIST

Many of you tell me about strange mists and shadows on your photographs. Paranormal or explainable?

Dear Jacky

A couple of years ago on a typical Sunday afternoon I had a strange experience. I was reading the paper and my eight-year-old daughter was in the room playing a game. I noticed that half of the room was filled with a white mist. It only lasted for a few seconds and I thought it was my eyes playing tricks on me until my daughter said, 'Mum, I've just seen that white mist again.' Then I knew that it wasn't my eyes playing tricks on me but something that just has no physical explanation.

Although she had seen the mist before she hadn't mentioned it, and she hasn't seen it since and neither have I.

Linda

Sometimes I see a white mist in my living room, too, but usually it is when the sun shines and I'm burning my incense! The same thing happened when my husband burned the potatoes … I'm teasing! The sunlight lit up the smoke which was already in the room, but this smoke could be something entirely different. Not every 'mist' experience is a ghost for sure, but maybe some are! What do you think?

PSYCHIC LIGHTS

Some write and tell me they have seen sparkling and coloured lights at the same time that they feel they are surrounded by the positive energy of their guardian angels. But are there other explanations? What are these lights?

Here is a letter about a white light experience. Did the bathroom mirror steam over or was something else going on here? It sounds as if Jay was receiving communication from a higher source as well as visits from her relatives.

> ***Hello there,***
> I have been married for almost 15 years. I am 30 years old and a very proud mother of five beautiful children. I am trying to find out some things that I really do not understand – well, not fully anyway – and I wanted to see if you think it is all normal and if others, too, experience all or any of the things that I have.

I see things and have done so for as long as I can remember. But it is only in the last few years I have really taken more notice. I am a little confused as to the way spirits will show themselves to us. I believe that they can appear as human forms, and also as energy … light perhaps? I may be totally wrong, but if I am seeing spirits this is the way they show themselves to me.

Gosh, where do I start? When I was a little girl I would have nightly visits from something which I still don't know to this day what it was. I do know that it was good and pure and of immense love.

It began with this brilliant white light (I guess this sounds like a movie, right?), but it's all true even if it may sound a little strange. I would see this white light in our bathroom mirror, every night while my parents and older siblings would be watching television. They all thought I was mad. I would lie in the doorway of our family room just staring into the bathroom for ages. I guess time seemed to stop and nothing else was real to me except this beautiful pure white light. It was so bright (kind of like the sun, but it never hurt to look into it). I never saw anyone, only this light, but I knew someone was there and they would talk with me but through my mind. And I would talk back also through my mind. I guess it would be called telepathy.

When this being told me it had to go, I would cry my eyes out. I would beg it not to go and my heart would just break. My family never understood why I would sob so hard over nothing; well, to them it was nothing! Mum was the only one who never doubted me. She would just comfort me.

When I was about 11 years old I saw a spirit in human form which I am sure was my grandfather, my mother's father. This scared the hell out of me at first and I ran like the wind straight up to the house to tell my mum. She brought out a photo of her dad, and it was him for sure.

Then, when I fell pregnant with my son Josh at the age of 16 years of age, I saw the most beautiful thing I have ever seen. My mum also saw this with me. We were lying in bed together and suddenly these balls of coloured light began floating around my room. They were unbelievable and the most magnificent colours, and they just floated all around the room. The feeling was of love.

Another time, I was watching television with my kids and I saw a blue 'star light' in the air about seven feet away from me, and then I asked in my head if it would please let me see it properly. I waited and waited and nothing happened so I started watching TV again and straight away I saw the star again but this time it lasted much longer. It was beautiful and all of a sudden it burst, like a starburst in the air and all this blue glitter went everywhere and then 'pow' it was gone. I instantly felt my heart jump with excitement and awe at what I had witnessed, and I felt very much privileged. I thanked it for sharing itself with me, too, even though that must sound strange to you!

Occasionally I hear disembodied voices and a lot of high-pitched ringing sounds in my ears. Sometimes it is painful. Sometimes it's not! I mainly hear voices at night but I can't always make out what they are saying. The women's voices sound louder than the men's.

I can sometimes hear the voices while I'm on the telephone talking to a friend, and when I ask my friends if they can hear someone else talking, too, they say no. I know it's not another line. How can it be possible to hear the same voices every time?

I just started up a meditation circle here in my home two weeks ago. I've had this nagging, pulling feeling to do this for years, but I never did, then all of a sudden this year it was like I just snapped and decided it's time. I have already got five people coming every week. I just love to see other people enjoy themselves and try and connect with their spirit guides.

Love and Light.

Jay, Australia

When readers experience anything which gives them pain of any sort, I always suggest they visit their medical doctor to rule out physical symptoms. It is sensible to check out any possible medical conditions first of all. I experience the whistling sensation myself sometimes and it is usually followed by some type of insight. I've also had my ears checked, though, just to be on the safe side!

'GHOST HUNTING' – A ROUGH GUIDE

If you haven't been ghost hunting and fancy a go, there are a few suggestions to make your evening fun and enjoyable. I know that many of my readers are fascinated by ghost hunting.

The idea is to investigate a 'haunted' location, a place (often an old building) where ghosts or spirits are regularly seen (thereby increasing your chances of seeing a ghost).

These few tips will keep you safe.

- Never explore a building or area without permission.
- Make sure that you work as a group – preferably with trusted friends.
- Old buildings may be unsafe – do make sure that the location has been checked in advance to ensure that no one falls down a big hole or through a ceiling, or trips over unsafe rubble.

Each member of your team should be armed with:

- a torch and spare batteries
- a walkie-talkie or mobile telephone (fully charged)
- food and drink
- warm, comfortable clothing (I would also suggest some sort of reflector strip like cyclists wear so that you can be found in the dark easily should an accident occur); gloves, hat (to protect your hair from insects and bats!)
- a camera … great for orb photography
- a notebook and pen to record any sightings – or a clipboard with prepared sheets ready to fill in the details (who had the sighting, what the vision looked like, etc.)
- a watch (for recording the time of any activities)
- specialist testing equipment (night-vision camera, voice-recording equipment, pendulum or dowsing rods, etc.)
- a map
- and, most important of all, a ghost-hunt partner.

Never wander around on your own in the dark, and arrange that members check in every 20 minutes or so with the group leader, reporting their location and activities. Make sure that, at all times, someone knows where you are. Better still: go on a ghost hunt organized by a professional company – who know what they are doing!

WHAT YOU ARE LOOKING FOR

Although it sounds obvious, the reason for your ghost 'hunt' is not to have an evening of fear but to locate signs of life after death. I personally prefer to communicate with spirits in the daylight, but apparently it's not so much fun! Light anomalies are more likely to occur at night, but as far as I am aware you don't really make more or better communication with a ghost after the 'witching hour' (midnight!). These are the things you might encounter on your hunt:

- cold spots – a sudden drop in temperature can indicate a spirit close by … or a draft
- orbs – these can sometimes be seen with the naked eye
- wailing sounds or screams (who ate the last bar of chocolate?)
- words (usually just one or two words – although this is rare)
- knocking, rappings
- things might be thrown or knocked
- sometimes heavier objects can be moved (a chair, for example – or a door might be closed by the spirit).

Recording equipment might pick up spirit sounds (known as Electronic Voice Phenomena or EVP), and don't forget to take regular photographs – especially if you feel a 'cold spot'!

Of course, for some people the haunted location is called 'home', and this is not so much fun for them. Let's address some of these problems.

GHOSTS IN A MODERN HOUSE

Dear Jacky

I live in Luton and we've lived in this house for five years. From the moment we moved in we began having strange experiences in the house. One night we heard a bedroom door slam and there were no windows open and no breeze in the house. My young children keep hearing 'me' calling them ... but it's not me!

Once I could smell a very strong perfume in the living room, and sometimes we feel uncomfortable in the house – it's just a feeling.

Strangely it's a brand new house, but we looked up the history of the land the house is built on. Two friends have told me that it was built on the entrance to a graveyard. When I moved in I didn't think I'd be able to stay here. I got holy water from the chapel and blessed the house myself. I did feel a little happier after I'd done that, but things still happen.

Jon, England

Hello, Jon

Many houses are 'haunted' but it is not necessarily a bad thing. Graveyards or not, even modern houses have spirits hanging around, and often the spirits are those of our loved ones on the other side.

If you want to keep the spirits away, may I recommend you 'smudge' your home using traditional smudge-sticks (sage wands) to cleanse the space in the house?

Sacred white sage is dried and tied into bundles. You light the end of the 'smudge' and move the smoke around the house. It's the smoke which cleanses and clears the house. (Buy from new age stores or the internet.)

Have you lost a loved one since living in the house? Does the perfume seem familiar? Next time you feel someone in the house, you could always say 'Hi'. Some people give their household spirits a fun name and it helps take the fear away. Mostly the spirits don't even know that you are there.

Remember, if the spirits are your loved ones they are just popping in to say hi and have a nose around the house – their love is as strong from the other side as it was when they were here, and they mean you no harm. You might not want to banish them.

Best wishes,

Jacky

HAUNTED HOUSE

Spirits (or ghosts) are more likely to haunt places than people, although this is a big concern of many. In the vast number of cases that people write to me about, the 'ghost' is really a spirit of someone they knew on Earth. The spirit is not haunting you but visiting you.

What's the difference between a ghost and a spirit?

Some people would say nothing, depending on your point of view, but I recognize a difference.

Spirits (as Souls) – Some Thoughts

Spirits are the souls of humans who once lived on the Earth plane (our level of existence). These souls have consciousness and are sometimes left in our atmosphere after they pass over. That is the fact, really – they don't fully pass over because they feel they have unfinished business on this side of life (maybe they were murdered and want to see justice; perhaps they are worried about loved ones still on this side of life). They don't want to leave … not just yet, anyway.

These souls can get almost trapped here because of their emotions which tie them to this side of life. (But not every spirit who is visiting is trapped.) Other souls come in a visitation (they visit a person or a location which was familiar to them when they lived here). These souls have full consciousness of who they are and who they were within their last human life, and often want to try and communicate with us, or at least let us know that they are around.

Their knockings and rapping can be terrifying but it's probably only Grandma saying, 'Hi there'!

Ghosts – Some Ideas

Ghost can be spirits held in our atmosphere who are unable to leave due to the trauma surrounding their death (maybe they are unaware that they have even died) or because they refuse to realize that they have to move on, and stay to be in a place they either loved or feel trapped in.

Ghosts can also be unconscious. Think of the way we record a voice on tape. Imagine now that during a moment of high emotion (a brutal killing, perhaps, or – at the other end of the emotional spectrum – maybe a lovely occasion like a wedding), the conditions are such that the energy of that moment is imprinted upon the atmosphere of the surroundings (for example, a building). I call this energy-memory.

It is no coincidence that large old buildings such as castles always seem haunted … especially during adverse weather conditions like thunder and lightning! The fact that a castle is often surrounded by water (a perfect conductor of electricity) combined with a lightning storm (electrical flashes in the air) make the conditions perfect to 'replay' that moment in time, that recording of a brief moment of high emotion: a soldier appears to walk through a wall or we see, for a moment, a woman who appears to be in agony simulating rocking a baby in a cot, who might well have passed over many years ago.

The memory seems forever etched into the very air around us. Buildings themselves seem to hold this energy, too, and many psychics are able to pick up on these memories trapped within the walls of an old place (using the psychic ability of touch, which is called *psychometry*). This recorded information can be held in other objects, too, like such as jewellery and furniture.

COMMON QUESTIONS

My daughters are often woken up by a woman who sits on the bed. The girls are terrified of this ghost and I don't know how to stop it happening.

Children are often frightened only because of the reaction of their parents (or they can scare each other). The most likely reason for the spirit awakenings is that the spirit wants to check on the children, or just wants to be seen or recognized.

The visitor might be a kindly woman who lived in the house previously (most likely dying there) or, as is usually the case, the spirit is actually a deceased relative.

If you tell your daughters that the spirit is probably their guardian angel (and the spirit is most likely to be keeping an eye on the children, so that's not a lie), then the girls will probably be quite happy about the visitor.

Perhaps next time the girls could ask the 'angel' her name. It could well turn out to be a great aunt or perhaps a grandmother who is checking on the little ones.

Whatever you do, don't appear frightened or concerned in any way. Your children will look to you for signs that everything is OK.

For more information, read my book *Angel Kids*, also published by Hay House.

Here's another letter extract:

My flatmate and I are not tidy guys. We leave our clothes all over the place, as most men do, but I have regularly woken up to find my clothes folded up in a neat pile by the bed. Now, I know *that I didn't do this, and my flatmate has experienced similar phenomena. We've both had doors opening and closing on their own (or unlocking) and have both heard strange noises.*

To be honest, we were both getting a bit freaked out about the whole thing, so when I saw the previous owner at the supermarket last week I asked her about it. Once I explained what was happening she just went, 'Oh, so it's happening to you, too.' I was cross that she hadn't told me the house was haunted before, but it turns out that a friend of her son's killed himself in the house. Help!

This is very frustrating for you all … including the spirit. This type of ghost activity is often called poltergeist, which translates as 'noisy ghost'. This spirit is literally trying to attract your attention and probably has no idea that he has died. He is wondering why no one is speaking to him any more.

I would suggest you call in an expert, either someone from your church (most churches have departments which deal with spirit activity) or a medium (a psychic who can communicate with the dead) trained in clearing spirits from a property. Ask at your local Spiritualist church to see if they have a specialist who can handle this for you – or try your local new age shop to see if they know anyone who could help.

This family had real problems:

My mother has recently bought an old house and, although we thought it was very pretty, now that she has moved in the energy of the house has changed so much. The property has a 'stagnant' quality to it. We all feel tired and even frightened there, but have no idea why. Might there be a ghost? Can you help?

A home can often hold the energy of its previous owners (and that might include any rows they've had!) and although you aren't going to start knocking down doors and walls, you can make a few little changes and alter the entire energy of the home.

This is the modern, Western version of the ancient art of placement (to create positive chi/energy), Feng Shui. Try as many of the following as are possible:

- Remove and destroy or clean old carpets and rugs.
- Clean the whole house from top to bottom – call in other family members for back-up. Make sure windows, the insides of cupboard and light fittings are all tackled.
- Decorate where possible (paint everything – or at least paint walls in the worst rooms). Go for light colours (cream or soft white will make a massive change).
- Remove drawer lining paper (or replace), take down old wallpapers; remove newspapers (sometimes left under rugs or carpets).
- Open windows – all of them, and let the fresh air circulate.
- Use an oil burner and infuse natural aromatherapy oils into the house (following manufacturer's instructions). Orange and lemon oils are lovely for 'cutting through' any negative 'vibes'. Try lavender, too.
- Bring fresh flowers and plants into the house (some Feng Shui experts suggest you don't have plants in smaller bedrooms because they release small amounts of CO_2, although I've never had a problem with this myself).

- Paint the front door a fresh bright colour and place pots of flowers each side of the door.
- Have the previous owners left furniture in the home? Consider selling this (especially if it's not to your taste).
- Remove clutter (inside and out).
- Have curtains professionally cleaned (although simple cotton, unlined curtains will probably be fine in your washing machine).

I'm sure you will find that these simple steps, or as many as you can do, will make a massive difference to the feel of the energy in your mother's home, and the energy of the previous owners (both living and deceased) will soon disappear. Clean … to clear.

Here's another one:

Ever since my teenage son went on a ghost hunt he has been terrified to sleep at night. He and his friends messed around with a Ouija board, and my son says that something 'attached' itself to him and is following him around. I am at my wits' end and don't know what to do about it.

This can be a problem – not spirit attachment so much as people thinking that they are possessed or that something is 'with' them. The likelihood of spirit attachment of this type is extremely rare and nearly always in the mind (every creaking door or flashing light becomes a 'ghost' … it isn't). This can be a particular problem with teenagers or the elderly – anyone who is vulnerable or suffering from depression or stress might take on the 'symptoms' of a non-existent spirit.

A Ouija board (or angel board) can be a wonderful tool for safely connecting to loved ones on the other side – but, like a car being driven by someone who is not experienced, it can also be a dangerous tool.

Although I wouldn't say that there are lots of 'bad' spirits hanging around, there are annoying, pesky ones who are keen to scare teenagers and stop them messing around. This can be a frightening business, and really all spirit contact should be performed with love and respect. When it isn't, this is where problems can occur.

It's unlikely that your son will be comforted by you saying this, and I suggest you get an expert in to speak to him. Some mediums deal with this type of phenomenon and would be able to reassure him that nothing has followed him home. Perhaps the medium would be prepared to perform some sort of 'clearing ceremony' to set his mind at rest. Do check to see if there is a charge for this service, and if possible try and get a recommendation from a friend or meet the person in advance to make sure you feel comfortable about the whole thing.

The best 'cure' for this type of thing is just not to mess about in the first place – easier said than done, I know! Ouija boards can be very accurate and teens will ask silly questions like 'When will I die?' Of course it's just as likely that the spirit entity operating the board will be an irritating energy who is keen to frighten those working the board … giving ridiculous and untrue answers.

So be warned, all teenagers out there: leave séances to the professionals.

Here is another snippet from my postbag:

My two-year-old has been talking to a ghost for about 12 months now – almost as soon as she could speak she started chatting to someone who wasn't there (well, we couldn't see it, anyway).

Now she has begun giving us messages from this ghost and telling us what he looks like. To be honest, he does sound a little like my Uncle Bob, who died when I was younger. Should I be encouraging my daughter in this or not? I don't want people to think she is weird.

Many children can see things that adults cannot, and this is a growing phenomenon. In nearly every case the visiting spirit is a deceased family member or friend. The two realms (heaven and Earth) really are getting closer together, and more spirits than ever are able to reach out to us.

Wouldn't it be fun to see if the 'ghost' really is Uncle Bob? Do you (or a family member) have a photograph of him? Don't say anything to your daughter but you could leave the photograph out on a table (along with other old photographs) and see if she notices. If not, then don't mention it at all.

You don't need either to encourage or discourage the contact; as long as it isn't causing any problems, you can let her get on with it.

Some children do lose this ability as they get older so, may I suggest you write down any communications or messages that you remember and then start 'casually' to record any new ones? Your daughter might be interested in this when she gets older.

And another:

Sometimes we have lights flicker in our house or the television goes off and on (or changes channels) on its own. My husband thinks this is a ghost. Do we have anything to worry about?

Some spirits do manipulate electrical items to attract our attention – but it's just as likely that the flickering is due to natural variations in the electrical current or that the TV could be faulty! Not every activity in the house is paranormal phenomena … but it might be.

Having said that, the spirits of our loved ones do use these 'tricks' to let us know they are around (but there are many different types of phenomena that happen, so these would probably be accompanied by more 'signs'.

In short, there is nothing to worry about at all – these are expressions of loving contact!

I am concerned because there is an old deserted house up the road and some kids have found a way of getting inside. My kids are up there a lot and my neighbour says it's haunted. Should I keep the kids away?

You have more to fear from the danger of the house itself. Deserted homes can be very dangerous places, so do try and track down the owners, or just contact your local council or police station and see if someone can make the building secure again. In the meantime, yes, keep your children away from the house, and perhaps mention this to other parents if possible. Ghosts are the least of your worries!

Chapter 10

Your Quick Questions

'There is a theory which states that if ever anybody discovers exactly what the Universe is for and why it is here, it will instantly disappear and be replaced by something even more bizarre and inexplicable. There is another theory which states that this has already happened.'

Douglas Adams

Some questions come up in my post bag over and over again. Let's whiz through these quickly.

A psychic once told me that I have a guardian angel. I love this idea, can it really be true?

Yes, we all have a guardian angel or spiritual guide who works with us from the other side of life.

What is the role of a guardian angel?
The role of your guardian angel is to love, protect and guide you on your life mission.

'Angels have no philosophy but love.'
Adeline Cullen Ray

How do I find out the name of my guardian angel?
Ask your guardian angel to bring you a sign. You might get several 'coincidences' where you hear or see the same name over and over again. You can also ask for your angel's name in a dream or during meditation.

What happens if I don't get or can't hear my angel's name?
Guardian angels don't always have a name in the way that we might understand it. They are often known by their attributes and/or personalities. Of course it's OK for you to give your guardian angel a name. Make one up!

How do I get close to my guardian angel? What exactly do I have to do?
Although lots of people have written books full of ideas about how to do this (including me), there is no strict set of rules to follow. Bringing angels into your life is about being open to their love and support. Meditating is a good way of becoming more aware.

You can read about angels, use angel cards (divination cards with motivational sayings and words of assurance), create rituals or make displays of angel-inspired items (figurines, crystals, candles, etc.), decorate your home or workspace with angel products and wear angel-decorated clothing and jewellery. The list is endless.

Can anyone work with angels?
Yes. You just have to want to work with them. Invite them into your life today.

I want to work with my guardian angel but I can't hear or feel anything. Have I done something wrong?
No, not at all. Angels are subtle in their approach. They don't want to frighten us. As we grow in confidence their messages become less subtle and more clear.

How can I meet my guardian angel?
A great way of doing this is to use a guided meditation recording. I have created one of my own, but lots of angel teachers produce them. My CD is actually called 'Meet Your Guardian Angel' (*see* the Further Resources chapter). On it I've recorded a 'visual journey' with background music, and I talk you through an imagined walk to a special place where your angel is waiting to talk to you. You create the whole thing in your head.

Don't think for one minute that it's all make-believe – the imagination opens many doors! Oh, and listen through headphones for maximum effect.

I believe in angels, but my family tease me about this. How do I convince them that angels are real?
Don't try! Each person walks his own spiritual path and discovers things in his own individual way. You don't have to prove your beliefs or even justify them in any way.

If you feel you need to explain a little you could say that:

- Human bodies have very limited abilities when it comes to perceiving the world around them. (We can't see X-rays, radio waves and any number of things we know exist. If it vibrates at a fast enough speed, like the blades of a fan, then we can't see it … even though we know it's there.) Therefore, it makes no sense to base our belief system on what we can see alone.
- There are literally millions of documented cases of angel encounters, and these stories come from all over the world.
- Not all experiences happen to one person – sometimes there are several witnesses.
- Why would people lie about something which might open them to ridicule?

How do we know that heaven really exists?
Lots of different ways. Many believe on faith alone, but you don't have to. People all over the world have been through near-death experiences (lifting out of their bodies at the point of physical death and ending up in the heavenly

realms before being sent back to their earthly bodies again because 'it's not their time' to die). So people have been to heaven and then come back to tell us all about it.

Millions have experienced deceased loved ones appearing in dreams and visions. Sometimes these spirits will explain or even show those left behind what it's like in heaven. Mediums (those with the ability of communicating with spirits) are also told – or shown – what it's like on the other side, too.

Some hypnotherapists take their patients into deep hypnotic trance-states where they recall their heavenly homes – the place where they existed before being born. There are hypnotherapists with thousands of cases on file from people who don't know each other and couldn't possibly have compared notes.

Are angels born here on Earth as children? A child I know is perfect in every way – she has to be an angel!

The planet Earth is going through big changes at the moment … a spiritual transition. Many advanced beings from other worlds are being incarnated at this time (but of course they look just the same as we do, born into normal human bodies). They are being born at this time in history so that they can help humanity.

I have received thousands of letters from around the world from parents with children who have exceptional psychic ability and have experienced unbelievable paranormal events.

You can read more about this fascinating phenomenon in my book *Angel Kids*.

A psychic told me that the Archangel Michael is working with me. Would Michael be my guardian angel?
No. The Archangels are powerful and majestic beings who work on very high levels. They are in charge of planets, bodies of water, weather, etc. However, having said that, they do still work with human souls, too. They generally appear when requested by our guides, or we can ask them to intervene in difficult situations as well. You will have your own guardian angel, too.

I feel bad asking a great Archangel to help me – won't they be busy doing more important things like stopping wars?
Angels are not limited by time and space in the way that we are. They can be in many places at once, so ask away. I can't promise they will solve every problem, but they will help whenever they can.

My husband and I are struggling with money at the moment. I have asked my guardian angel to bring me some money, but no one has given me any. I did get a small promotion at work recently, but this is not enough extra money. Why am I being ignored?
You're not! Our role on Earth is to learn and grow through the acts that we perform in the great play of life. When we are short of money it usually means one of two things: 1.

We spend too much (that's most of us) or 2. We need to earn more. The choices are ours.

Have a look at your budget (and if you don't work with a budget, start one today). We all need to live within our means – that is a lesson that many of us are struggling with this lifetime around.

Of course you can always make more money if you prefer. Can you sell things? Get another part-time job? Move to a smaller house or a cheaper neighbourhood? Or maybe set up your own business? By all means ask your guardian angel to help you – the whole thing works best when they are helping us to create positive change in our lives rather than just expecting them to solve every single problem.

If our guardian angels sorted everything out, they would be stunting our growth as spiritual beings. The best teachers help their pupils to be independent and do things for themselves.

'There are two tragedies in life. One is not to get your heart's desire. The other is to get it.'

George Bernard Shaw, *Man and Superman*

Could my guardian angel be my grandmother who died before I was born?

Our angel or guide is normally a friend or teacher we have known from other lifetimes … a more advanced soul. Their role is to help us to achieve life goals and complete tasks we have chosen before we were born. Therefore it is harder for a family member to perform this role. They struggle with being objective, and want to protect us at every turn.

Having said that … my own spirit guide has taken a back seat and permitted several of my own deceased relatives (my father, uncle and father-in-law) to help guide me because their communication is clearer to me. So the short answer is yes, it's possible, but it's unusual. If your grandmother has chosen to help you, then she won't be working alone. You'll have a guide, too.

Would my grandmother still be aware of what is going on in my life now she is in heaven?
Absolutely yes, if she has an interest in your life then she can pop in from time to time and check on your progress.

Would my late father be aware of my two boys who were born after he died?
Yes. If he chooses, he can see them, and probably will already have seen them. Remember he will probably have met their souls (or already know their souls) before they were born. He may have seen them before you did!

Can my late mother help me with my life problems now that she has passed over?
She can and she probably will. Our deceased relatives are not terribly objective (it's not easy to sit back and watch us

make mistakes – even if those mistakes would help us to learn a lesson). However, I have many case histories on file of people who've had help from deceased relatives.

Some people hear the voice of a loved one, which helps to prevent an accident. Others see deceased relatives when they are unconscious, and those relatives can literally push their soul back into their bodies … if it's not their time to die.

Would my child, who died as a baby, be an angel now?
Not in the traditional sense of the word. This is a Victorian idea. In earlier history our ancestors lost many babies in their early years. This is where the concept of 'cherubs' comes from (babies with wings!).

However, the spirit of your child will be in heaven and is being looked after – sometimes by deceased relatives or, when none is available, by those who have chosen this special role. I have many stories on file which illustrate this fact (folk whose loved ones have visited them in dream visitations have brought the baby with them to provide reassurance that the baby is safe).

My aunt was rubbish at giving advice in life and she has appeared in a dream to advise me. Should I listen to her?
As with all things in life, we have free will and freedom of choice in how we live our lives. You are the ultimate decision maker. Your aunt will have a broader perspective

than she did when she was alive, for example more information will be available to her, but she won't have suddenly become an all-seeing, all-knowing being.

Listen to the advice and use it … it if feels right; or ignore it if you want to – it's your choice.

A deceased friend has appeared in a dream to warn me to be careful about the man I am seeing, as she doesn't trust him. Would my spirit friend lie to me?
I doubt it. It takes a lot of effort and energy to make an appearance like this, so no doubt your late friend has her reasons. In my experience of afterlife communication, spirits bring messages of love and comfort.

Be a little cautious about your new male friend just in case – it won't hurt to stay alert.

What sort of signs might I expect from my loved ones that they are still around me?
There are as many different signs as there are people. The signs will often be meaningful to you even if their messages mean nothing to others. These signs might include the appearance of white feathers, lights flickering, electrical items switching themselves on and off, clockwork items playing when they haven't been wound up, bells, doorbells and alarms ringing when they have not been pushed or set, and the deceased appearing in 'dreams' and during meditation.

When my dad appeared in a dream vision after he died, he appeared younger than when he died. Why was this?
Our loved ones often appear young, fitter and 'in their prime' when they visit us in this way. As souls they don't have bodies in the way that we do, so can choose to show themselves in any way they wish. People with missing limbs in life will appear whole; those with short hair who always wanted long, glossy hair may appear with that, and people with mental disorders appear in perfectly normal mental health (although this perfect wellness may build over time and over several spirit visits: your loved one might at first appear with some of the ailments cured, then next visit they are better still, and so on).

Why does it take so long for some family members to go into the light?
I assume you mean because you can feel your loved one around after they have died? Usually our loved ones go straight to the heavenly realms but will often hang around (coming back with a guide or guardian) for a few days so that they can be reassured their loved ones on Earth are OK.

They do worry about us once they pass on, but they don't have the same feelings of grief as we do, because they know we will all be together again.

Of course, souls have a choice and may decide they are not ready to leave for a while. Some souls do not immediately realize they have died, and this can also hold them back a few days or so.

Why is it that some souls don't pass over right away and get trapped in limbo?
Imagine a sudden and unexpected death … probably with no pain. The soul 'wakes up' in a new form, but life around him looks the same except no one can hear him – no matter how hard he tries to speak to people around him. He has passed over but the journey was so subtle he has not yet realized he has died (what a lovely way to pass). His soul can see life much as before, but no one he knows can see him. He can't attract their attention because it's his spirit which is trying to communicate.

Guardians and other deceased loved ones have come to collect the departed soul. They're calling out 'Hey, friend, we're over here … come to the light … ' but the departed soul is still concentrating on the earthly plane and doesn't notice!

Don't worry – in time they realize and go on their way

What will have happened to my dog after she died?
Pet souls also leave the body and are escorted to the heavenly realms. Pets can stay with the human souls who loved them on Earth, now that they are both on the other side (if this is what both of them want) or they can be cared for by human souls who have chosen this role (the

role of caring for spirit pets). Once we are both on the other side we can visit our pets and they us – if we wish.

'All animals, except man, know that the principal business of life is to enjoy it.'
Samuel Butler, *The Way of All Flesh*

I hated my uncle. When I die will I have to see him again?
No, not if you don't want to, although part of the learning and growth of human souls is that we learn to understand each other, and forgiveness is part of that. If another human being has hurt you in life, their own progress may be impeded on the other side. Part of the growth of both of you is that you both work to make things right between you.

We don't always understand the reasons why things happen the way they do. Your uncle may have taken on the role of someone mean to help you to become stronger! (It sounds like a poor excuse, though, doesn't it?). When you yourself cross over (at some distant future date) you will understand this better.

In my youth I made many mistakes and hurt a lot of people. Will I go to hell when I die?
Only a hell of your own making! Forgive yourself and put things right now. We all make mistakes and this is part of being human. Apologize where you can and, where this is

not possible, help others instead. It's never too late to turn your life around.

My mother took her own life. What will have happened to her when she passed over? Will she be punished?
Taking your own life is considered a terrible waste of a human body. Souls who 'cross themselves over' almost always regret what they have done (although not every case is the same and souls who are in great pain and close to death may be viewed more leniently). They realize that the lessons they have escaped still have to be learned. In other words, they have to come back and learn the same lessons in another life and in a different body at some future date.

Your mother will have full awareness at this point of how her actions have affected the choices of others she left behind. It's painful to see how we may have hurt those on Earth by our actions. You mother won't be punished but she may at first have suffered anguish at her 'choice'.

She will be supported, loved and helped to make better choices next time. The pain she suffers will only be of her own creation, and with time she will learn to forgive herself. Time is a great healer and in other lives many of us will have made the same mistake.

'The greatest of victories is the victory over oneself.'
Dhammapada ***(Buddhist collection of sacred texts) 103-5***

Is it true that when we die we have a 'past life review'? That we have to see our life (the life we've just lived) in front of us?
Yes indeed. We see the life we have just lived in every detail. Many who go through near-death experiences tell us how they 'review' things that have happened in their lives that they've completely forgotten. It happens at super-fast speed, but this doesn't stop us seeing every detail. We can slow down certain aspects of this 'review' if we wish, and look at them more clearly.

So … it's like we live the life all over again?
Not really. It's like a 'super-aware' version of the life we've just lived. We see the life, re-experience our thoughts and feelings, and feel and sense the thoughts and feelings of those we have touched during our lifetime. If you were kind to someone, for instance, you will actually 'feel' the emotion that you created in that person.

If you shouted at someone or hurt them you will literally feel that emotion, too. Some people find they even enter into the action of their life in a way they never did during their lifetime.

You may also experience the 'ripple effect' caused by the positive and negative actions of your life. For example if you kicked a dog, the dog may go on and bite someone. You would also feel the pain of this person if your action inadvertently caused suffering in others (positive effects are experienced, too).

What is the purpose of the past life review?
It gives us the opportunity of checking out how well we did, what lessons we learned and those that we have to work on more in other lives. For those who have seen the review during a near-death experience, it gives them the opportunity of working on their mistakes and correcting wrongdoings they have made already – once they return to their body.

Ultimately we can all do this – even if we haven't had a past life review. Inside, most of us know that we can be unkind on occasion and can work harder to make sure this doesn't happen.

'The unexamined life is not worth living.'
Socrates

This is a big question, but what is the purpose of life?
The answer is fairly simple, really: to learn and grow as a human soul; to help others as you do so; to love one another; to know that ultimately we are all ONE; to eventually return to the source (God); to be grateful for this amazing opportunity of living an earthly life with all the wonders it brings.

How can I thank my angels for all the help they have given me in my life? I am so grateful.
Help others as you have been helped.

'We make a living by what we get,
we make a life by what we give.'
Winston Churchill

How can I tell the difference between an ordinary dream about my deceased mother and a real visit from her spirit? I often dream about her but I'm not sure if it's a real experience or not.

There are several ways of telling the difference:

1. A dream 'visitation' (that which we call a visit from spirit) will seem more real than a dream. You will be lucid and aware during the experience.
2. You will recall the experience when you wake up – although not all the details of what you spoke about. The memory will remain with you for many years.
3. The person will appear in good health (usually), often look younger and in their prime of life. Sometimes people describe their loved ones as 'glowing with health' or 'fizzing with energy'.
4. There may be other living or deceased relatives or friends with you during the visitation experience (if living, sometimes they will actually recall having had a similar dream experience, but not always).
5. Sometimes you have to go 'upstairs' to see them (up in a lift, up an escalator or you meet in a dream multi-storey car park, for example). This is a visual way of showing you the levels between your dimension and theirs.

6. They may appear in a normal dream (i.e. you are dreaming and then they suddenly walk in and, at that point, it becomes a visitation and you become lucid and aware), or they may construct a specific setting for you to meet (an old house you both knew, a bar you used to meet up in, etc.).
7. You are likely to say ' … but you're dead, aren't you?' (or a similar phrase) and point out the obvious because the visitation is a real experience as you consciously remember that they have passed on. This initially confuses you.
8. It's possible on occasion to feel a hug or get a kiss from them. These experiences feel very real, unlike in a normal dream.
9. They bring messages of love and reassurance.
10. For more detail on this phenomenon, check out my book *Angels Watching Over Me*.

What sort of message might my grandmother bring me if she did visit me in a dream?
Messages in dream visitations are usually very similar: I love you; I miss you; everything will be OK; everything will work out; I am watching over you; I am your guardian angel; I am proud of you.

Sometimes our loved ones may bring an answer to a question we have been asking: 'The will is hidden in the back of the desk'; 'You will get the new job/pass your test';

'I died of a weak heart and nothing sinister'; 'I love my new baby grandson and have visited him'; 'This is the name of the person who killed me' (seriously – someone told me they had a dream visitation like this once!).

I want to teach others about angels and run workshops and classes. Do I need a qualification?

No, but if you take a few angel classes yourself it will help you to become a better teacher. Teaching/training is a skill in itself, so do look into it thoroughly. You may also find counselling skills useful. Of course, if you attend a few angel workshops by other teachers it will help you to decide on your own approach. I run workshops myself, as do many established angel experts.

In the meantime, read everything you can get your hands on and then, when you feel ready, just start. The teacher learns best by teaching.

You can practise on your friends first of all, and be at peace knowing you are working in one of the most exciting fields around – helping people to open their eyes to the hidden worlds and discovering that we are souls in a human body on a life journey. It's a wonderful feeling when people discover for the first time that they are always supported and loved by their angels.

Each teacher works in his own way, and I am sure you will find your own unique path.

I work as a healer and I often get messages for people whom I treat. Should I pass these on?
Only if you advise the person in advance that this might happen and they agree to a message. Your intent might be positive but I feel it's unethical to give readings in this way without prior consent.

Of course, many of your clients will be delighted with a message, but always check first.

I sometimes see spirits and angels and they appear to me as white smoke. Why is this?
Angels appear to different people in different ways. Some see beings of light, others see sparkling lights or balls of energy. On rarer occasions it's possible to see a clear vision of the angels as a human-like being (a light-being) with wings. Yet others see angels as solid humans without wings.

Your spirits are not smoke (which would need a flame to be created) but I believe you are seeing a type of astral mist. In ghosts this material is called ectoplasm.

Do angels have wings? My little girl saw an angel with wings, but I read that angels don't have them.
Some people see wings and others do not. Strictly speaking, they don't have physical bodies so can appear to us any way they want to. The idea of wings is a human creation. Because of the speed at which angels can appear and disappear, early humankind believed that angels would

need wings like birds to enable them to fly … but of course they don't.

'The reason angels can fly is because
they take themselves lightly.'
G. K. Chesterton

I have always sensed angels around me but I want to develop my ability. Any suggestions?
Yes, meditate.

My son needs all the help he can get at the moment. Would it be OK to ask angels to help him?
Yes, it would. You can ask your own guardian angel to assist your son's guardian, or ask for one of the Archangels. If in doubt ask for 'the angel who can most help in this situation and attend to his needs', and know that the right angel will be sent. Know that it will be done.

Remember that your son's problems may be related to his very own life lessons. Your angels cannot take away the lesson but they can usually help … as long as it's in your son's best interests that they do so. Your son, of course, has the option to refuse such help (as a human soul with free will.)

A friend of my mum's is so angry with me about my belief in life after death. I don't know what to say to him about it.
Be kind. Usually when someone is angry at you about the

belief that life goes on it's because they are suffering from a loss of their own. The anger is usually misdirected and comes as a result of grief.

What is your personal belief in the coming of the 'new age' and the so-called 'Earth changes'? I've read so much about the Earth blowing up or swivelling on its axis and so on. It's left me frightened by the whole thing.

Don't be frightened. We are all spirit living a human existence – whatever happens we will all be safe, as our souls will not be destroyed. Changes are happening around us. The planet is in trouble. Prince Charles gave a speech recently in Rio de Janeiro, to speak about '100 months to change the world'. He points out, as many have done before him, that we have damaged the planet almost beyond repair and that caring for the world must not become a 'luxury'.

Many believe, as I do, that we are being assisted by higher beings to make these necessary changes quickly. I believe that angels and guardians are raising the consciousness of humankind so that we may 'see' more clearly.

Our planet is a living, conscious being. It's time to stop fighting with each other and to begin loving and caring for our fellow human beings and the planet which gives us life … before it's too late.

* * * *

I have written about these subjects in more depth in many of my other books, so if you want more information please do check these out, too. (There is a full list of my books and CDs at the back of this book … and you can always check out your local library.)

Sadly it's time to move on to our final chapter. A treat of readers' experiences – to leave you thinking!

Chapter 11

Readers' Experiences

'There are more things in heaven and earth, Horatio,
Than are dreamt of in your philosophy.'
William Shakespeare, *Hamlet*

One of the best parts of my job is reading your amazing stories. So many of you have seen your loved ones, angels and guides all visiting from the other side, but have also had so many other 'paranormal happenings'. Even if there is only one 'weird' moment in your life – don't forget it … write it down! It shows that not everything is as we expect, not everything that happens in life fits into a neat little box.

Nothing happened yet? I bet it will now! Be open to every new experience that life brings. See the joy in life, both seen and hidden.

Nothing seems to be impossible these days. What is normal anyway? We all need a little reassurance and it always helps to hear what others are saying and experiencing. Most of the 'negative' encounters are only fear. When you look closely, most paranormal experiences are about love … or curiosity: one world searching to learn about another.

Let's look at a few more of your fascinating letters and stories … a real mixed bag.

ANGEL ON THE CEILING

Hi Jacky

A wonderful thing happened to me recently. I'd been feeling quite down with having a family of five children growing up. I just suddenly felt like someone had been by my side … and I saw a shadow but when I turned, no one was there. I sensed the 'someone' had a 'nice feeling' to them.

Last week when I got into bed I couldn't settle because I felt like someone was watching me. I would say they were at least 9 foot tall and I sensed them swooping over the ceiling right over the top of the bed (I saw nothing but couldn't take my eyes off the ceiling). I knew something was there. This happened two nights in a row and I felt so relaxed.

The weekend following this I went into a bookshop with my daughter and the first book I saw was your book, *An Angel Treasury*. I bought it and couldn't put it down and I read it in three days, which is quick for me with all these kids, washing, cooking, etc. Your books are fantastic and explain everything I want to know. You even write about feeling and sensing angels, which is what I think happened to me.

Thank you, Jacky, your books uplift me, so I have bought my sisters a copy each.

Tina, England

Dear Tina

I am honoured that you have been moved by my work. It's such a thrill as an author when your books 'hit the right spot'!

It certainly sounds like you are tuning in on your own guardian angel – trust your intuition, as I want all my readers to do. Our own energy field (the aura that surrounds our human bodies) can give us so much information. Animals are great at 'reading' people in this way. They immediately tune in to another animal's or human's energy field, before they look at the physical structure. Animals are more interested in how another body 'feels' than how it looks. (I'm sure they've got it right.)

If someone or something feels loving and positive – it probably is! Trust yourself and tune in to your sixth sense, which will only get stronger and stronger as time goes on.

Jacky

FROZEN TO THE SPOT

Hello, Jacky

This morning I had a funny experience. While I was in bed I turned over on to my stomach to have another ten minutes sleep, as I didn't have to get up for anything special. I then felt somebody sit on the bed on either side of me.

I couldn't turn over to see who it was, nor could I open my eyes. 'They' were there for about a minute, but I have no idea what it could mean. We have been in this house for 27 years and this is the first time something like this has happened. Were my angels trying to tell me something?

Thank you.

Susan, England

Susan is experiencing something called 'sleep paralysis'. Research suggests that this is a natural phenomenon: the body is paralysed during certain stages of sleep (REM sleep/dream sleep), a safety mechanism which prevents us harming ourselves by acting out the dream for real.

Occasionally something goes wrong and the mind awakens while the body is still in this paralysed state. This can create all sorts of hallucinatory-type experiences in the mind.

On the other hand, this is also a great time for our angels and the spirits of departed loved ones to visit us, too – and so visit they do! It is not uncommon for people to actually 'see', physically, their loved one or even hear their voice during this type of phenomenon. On occasion people will receive a visit from a guide or guardian, appearing from a brilliant white light, too.

Although these encounters sound terrifying, thankfully they are usually accompanied by tranquil feelings of peace and love.

I remember having had this experience myself, a few times. I thought I was totally awake but, although my mind was awake, my body couldn't move at all. The first time it happened I seriously thought someone was trying to smother me to death. They weren't!

On another occasion when my body was frozen, I 'saw' a little mouse jump up onto the bed and clean itself before jumping down onto the floor and running under the bed. The moment I could move I sat up in bed and switched on the light. I just knew that I had to find that mouse! Moments later it occurred to me that the mouse I'd seen was a cartoon mouse! Can you believe it? It felt so real, but of course, it can't have been!

Sleep paralysis has been blamed for many of the alien-abduction experiences that are supposed to have occurred. Maybe this is the case, but I would never rule out the possibility that some of the experiences where people have encountered beings from outer space just might be true!

Hi Jacky

My name is Janice and I am 48 years old. During the Christmas period I had a strange thing happen to me and I'm wondering if I can get any help explaining it.

My husband and I had our granddaughter Paige stay overnight. She is four. We spoil her rotten (the result of having three sons, I guess) and we often let her sleep between us. It was about 1.15 a.m.; Paige and her granddad were fast asleep. I had my back to our bedroom door and I don't think I was completely asleep. I felt strange ... like I was sleepy but not actually asleep. I was aware that someone came into the room and leaned on the bed behind me. I felt the pressure of the bed go down, ever so slightly, nothing heavy. I felt like someone was watching us. I tried and tried with all my might to wake up, trying to force my eyes open, but I couldn't. I couldn't speak either (I wanted to call out).

I was trying to move to touch my husband to tell him, but I couldn't. Just then I felt the 'dip' in the bed go and I heard footsteps running across the landing, very lightly again, definitely not heavy enough to be my 18-year-old son, who was fast asleep in another room.

I forced my eyes open, afraid that Paige was out of bed in the dark, but she lay beside me fast asleep, oblivious to what had just happened. I lay and listened for a while; I was a little afraid, before I plucked up the courage to get out of bed and take a look around. Everything seemed quite normal, but I couldn't go back to sleep because of what I had experienced.

Our house is not really old, although we have lived here for almost 26 years. The previous owners didn't lose anyone here. The house is built on old capped mine shafts and grassy banks. I don't know if there is any explanation for what I experienced, but it was quite real for me.

Janice, Wales

Isn't it strange how similar this little experience is to the one before? Some people do believe that spirits visit during the night. It certainly feels as if they do, so I like to keep an open mind. During one of my own sleep paralysis experiences I remember trying to call out for my husband and my voice sounded as if it were in a different dimension! It echoed, as if I were standing in some sort of cave! Strange!

ANGEL FEATHER ... FOR MY DOG?

Hi Jacky

I just have to share this with you; I don't know if it was an angel or not ... here goes!

Last night a friend of ours came round for tea. He had to have one of his dogs put to sleep a few weeks ago and we were talking about it. I used to own a beautiful Staffordshire bull terrier myself, who sadly died four years ago.

I was telling my friend how much I missed our dog and showed him a poem called 'Rainbow Bridge', which is a lovely poem basically saying that we will meet our beloved pets again when the time comes. We are having our living room decorated at the moment so we have no furniture in there apart from the sofa. I reached down to the floor to pick up my glass of wine, and there was this tiny white feather next to my glass! I picked it up and said, 'I wonder if this is an angel?'

I held the feather for a little while and, when I looked closer, the tip of the feather was red. It reminded me that my little Staffy was red. I put the feather down on the settee and went to bed. When I went downstairs this morning, I looked for the feather and it had gone.

Also to top it off, I walked into the showroom at work this morning and the song that was on the radio was 'Eternity' by Robbie Williams, which was the song that was on when the vet rang to tell me that Staffy had died!

Love,

Hannah, England

These little 'coincidences', or synchronicities, often build up to create a picture where it seems as if something magical is going on. Don't you think that it was the perfect time to remind Hannah that life goes on, even for pets? I am sure she was comforted by the experience.

SOUTH AFRICA BUSINESS FEATHER

Jacky

First, Jacky, thank you for the 'platform' where we can share our experiences; I know it must help a lot of people. I've had a couple of angelic encounters and can let you know about them in due course. The one that stands out most in my mind is the following.

I worked at a company where a lot of the staff members were not very happy. Management was very dictatorial and suspicious of everything. We had a particular person who worked extremely hard and long hours in a managerial position. His name is Craig and there was a very tense relationship between him and the managing director of the company.

Without boring everyone, the quick version of the story is that eventually there was a stand-off between the two of them and Craig was suspended from work (pending a disciplinary hearing) and subjected to the humility of not being allowed on the premises of the company unless specifically asked to be there. He also had his office keys taken away from him. Just so you know, I do not think I have come across someone who was more scrupulously honest than Craig and the whole thing seemed unjust to me.

The day of the hearing came and I told Craig that the angels would be present. In a closed building in an industrial area of the city, suddenly a feather came floating from the floor above where I was sitting. It was also seen by a big burly courier who came to our office and said to me, 'I see the angels are here.' Having been a believer for a long time, I was surprised to hear this comment from him. He confirmed that he could feel their presence and that they were obviously sorely needed that day. After he left the office I quickly looked for the feather, but never found it.

The outcome was positive: Craig was paid off by the company, but went on to become the managing director of a very good international concern, representing the company throughout South Africa and neighbouring countries. All I can say is 'Thank You, Angels' – and thank you to facilitators such as yourself and for all your books. I have a host of them with me all the time.
Ann, South Africa

Hi Ann
Thank you so much for sharing this story, and for permission to publish it. It's unusual to receive stories like this one (that are business related), so it's nice to see a few more like yours just beginning to sneak into my postbag.

I am thrilled that you have enjoyed my books and that they help you. There are a few of us spreading the angelic message now. The more the merrier!
Jacky

Sadly it's the end of the book. I want to thank you for coming on this journey with me. It's lovely to make new friends and I hope we meet again in other books. There's just time for one more question …

THE FINAL QUESTION AND THE FINAL ANSWER

Are angels and the afterlife real? Does it all exist … in your opinion?

I can only answer in my personal opinion, but I have been studying these phenomena for a very long time. I've read accounts from ancient texts, books about near-death and afterlife visits; I've talked with scientists, doctors and counsellors and read and interviewed thousands about their own personal experiences as well as experiences with angels and the afterlife personally.

Dad, father-in-law Jack and Uncle Eric – my three angels – continue to visit me personally from the other side of life, and no doubt their influence in my future books will be obvious to all.

It's real!

* * * *

My own knowledge of the 'what is' has grown so much over the years, thanks mainly to the stories my readers send me from all over the globe ... thousands of them!

I always say that piecing together the life in the world hereafter is like putting together a jigsaw puzzle – and I've always loved a good puzzle! I don't yet have all the answers (and maybe I never will), but I do believe I have a good few pieces of the puzzle joined together – along with some of the straight edges.

I hope you have enjoyed my book – I have many more you may not have seen yet (listed at the back of this one). Try your local library as well as your local bookshop – and you can also order personally signed copies at my website.

If you have experiences of your own, or just a question that I haven't answered here, then I would love to hear from you. Please feel free to write to me via my publishers. I welcome all your letters, cards and gifts (I treasure them all).

You can also reach me by filling in the form on my website (www.AngelLady.co.uk). I do try and answer every single question personally.

I also give many talks and workshops around the country. Perhaps we will meet one day. Please come and introduce yourself and say hello.

Take care,

Jacky x

Also Available from Jacky Newcomb

Books by Jacky

An Angel Treasury (Harper Element, 2004)

A Little Angel Love (Harper Element, 2005)

An Angel Saved My Life (Harper Element, 2006)

An Angel by My Side (Harper Element, 2006)

An Angel Held My Hand (Harper Element, 2007)

A Faerie Treasury (Hay House, 2007)

Angels Watching Over Me (Hay House, 2007)

Angel Kids (Hay House, 2008)

DVD

Angels – produced by New World Music

CDs

Meet Your Guardian Angel (guided meditations) – produced by Paradise Music

Healing with Your Guardian Angel (guided meditations) – produced by Paradise Music

Angel Workshop (workshop with meditations) – produced by Paradise Music

Crystal Angels (instrumental by Llewellyn, cover notes by Jacky – produced by Paradise Music)

Jacky is a regular contributor to many magazines and has several regular columns including those in these journals:

Soul & Spirit (Angel Answers)

Chat – It's Fate (Dear Angel Lady)

SimplyHealth247

To contact Jacky, learn more about her work, request autographs, or to find out about talks and workshops:

Jacky Newcomb
c/o Hay House Publishers
292b Kensal Road
London W10 5BE
www.JackyNewcomb.com

You can also find her on Facebook and Twitter, too.

About the Author

Jacky Newcomb is an award-winning *Sunday Times* best-seller list author and a columnist, broadcaster, workshop tutor and speaker. Jacky regularly appears on TV as an expert on angels and the afterlife, including appearances on *This Morning* and *The Lorraine Kelly Show*.

Jacky is a columnist for the magazines *Chat – It's Fate*, *Soul & Spirit* and *Simply Health 247*. She writes on a wide range of issues including angels, the afterlife, paranormal and psychic subjects. Jacky has a special interest in the results of afterlife communication and how these affect healing and grieving in a positive way.

Jacky is a regular guest on local and national radio and is frequently interviewed in the national press including the *Daily Mail*, *Daily Mirror* and the *Daily Express*.

She has recently become a patron of the Youth Cancer Trust.

Notes

Notes

Notes

Hay House Titles of Related Interest

Angel Whispers, by Jenny Smedley

Ask Your Guides, by Sonia Choquette

Daily Guidance from Your Angels, by Doreen Virtue

Life-Changing Messages, by Gordon Smith

Why My Mother Didn't Want Me to Be Psychic,
by Heidi Sawyer

We hope you enjoyed this Hay House book.
If you would like to receive a free catalogue featuring additional Hay House books and products, or if you would like information about the Hay Foundation, please contact:

Hay House UK Ltd
292B Kensal Road • London W10 5BE
Tel: (44) 20 8962 1230; Fax: (44) 20 8962 1239
www.hayhouse.co.uk

***

Published and distributed in the United States of America by:
Hay House, Inc. • PO Box 5100 • Carlsbad, CA 92018-5100
Tel: (1) 760 431 7695 or (1) 800 654 5126;
Fax: (1) 760 431 6948 or (1) 800 650 5115
www.hayhouse.com

***

Published and distributed in Australia by:
Hay House Australia Ltd • 18/36 Ralph Street • Alexandria, NSW 2015
Tel: (61) 2 9669 4299, Fax: (61) 2 9669 4144
www.hayhouse.com.au

***

Published and distributed in the Republic of South Africa by:
Hay House SA (Pty) Ltd • PO Box 990 • Witkoppen 2068
Tel/Fax: (27) 11 467 8904
www.hayhouse.co.za

***

Published and distributed in India by:
Hay House Publishers India • Muskaan Complex • Plot No.3
B-2 • Vasant Kunj • New Delhi - 110 070
Tel: (91) 11 41761620; Fax: (91) 11 41761630
www.hayhouse.co.in

***

Distributed in Canada by:
Raincoast • 9050 Shaughnessy St • Vancouver, BC V6P 6E5
Tel: (1) 604 323 7100
Fax: (1) 604 323 2600

***

Sign up via the Hay House UK website to receive the Hay House online newsletter and stay informed about what's going on with your favourite authors. You'll receive bimonthly announcements about discounts and offers, special events, product highlights, free excerpts, giveaways, and more!
www.hayhouse.co.uk